"Frank Lachmann displays extraordinary musical acumen, from his evolutionary analysis of a baby's 1st 'Mmm' to his exploration of Beethoven's 9th. As a cabaret singer, I was taken by his insight into how Cole Porter's songwriting affirmed his sense of self despite agonizing pain and depression. In 'The Self-Restorative Power of Music' Yo-Yo Ma refers to 'goosebump moments'. During this time of isolation and shut-down of venues, I now experience those moments playing piano; yet I long to express myself again in halls filled with warm hearts and eager ears. To quote Frank Lachmann: 'I sing, therefore I am'."

KT Sullivan, *Artistic Director, The Mabel Mercer Foundation*

"This is a magnificent book written by a magnificent man who integrates so much about the human condition as it is encountered in music, in development, in the creation of meaning and in the psychoanalytic Spielraum. We are also treated as a contrapuntal motif to an intriguing inquiry into the complex logarithms that exist between Jewishness and music. This is a must read."

Jim Herzog, Training and Supervisory Analyst and
Child and Adolescent Supervisory Analyst, Boston,
Psychoanalytic Society and Institute,
Harvard Medical School

"Frank Lachmann's book offers a heady mixture of provocative ideas, striking insights, and deeply enjoyable and engaging personal reminiscences and reflections. Drawing on a wide range of disciplines— evolutionary biology, neuroscience, psychology, music theory, and more—his stimulating, persuasive exploration of musical meaning and the power of music to renew and transform both artist and audience make for a compelling reading. His lighthearted quasi-psychoanalyses of Wagner, Strauss, and Porter—speculating on the intersections between their lives and their art—are both entertaining and illuminating. Whether you're an experienced musician or a musical novitiate, this book will provide rewarding pleasure and rich food for thought."

David Shookhoff, Director of Education,
Manhattan Theatre Club

The Self-Restorative Power of Music

This book explores how we can understand the place of music from a self-psychological perspective, by investigating three journeys: the one we take when listening to music, the literal journey of the author from Nazi Germany to the United States, and the subjective round-trip between the past and the present.

Drawing on the work of Heinz Kohut, the author examines how music can provide us with a way to reconnect with a sense of self, and how this can manifest in psychological and physical ways. There is particular reference to the work of Richard Wagner, Cole Porter, and Richard Strauss, and an examination of how their music enabled them, in times of stress and crisis, to restore and maintain a more positive sense of self. Finally, the book looks back at the author's own experiences of music and the place of music in the Jewish world.

With clinical excerpts, personal narrative, and sophisticated psychoanalytic insights, this book will appeal to all psychoanalysts wanting to understand the place of music in shaping the psyche, as well as music scholars wishing to gain a deeper appreciation of the psychology of music.

Frank M. Lachmann, Ph.D., a psychoanalyst and Founding Faculty of the Institute for the Psychoanalytic Study of Subjectivity is author or co-author of more than 160 journal publications and books. He is the sole author of *Transforming Aggression* and *Transforming Narcissism* and honorary member of the Vienna Circle for Self-Psychology, the William Alanson White Society, and the American Psychoanalytic Association.

Psychoanalytic Inquiry Book Series
Joseph D. Lichtenberg

Series Editor

Like its counterpart, *Psychoanalytic Inquiry: A Topical Journal for Mental Health Professionals*, the Psychoanalytic Inquiry Book Series presents a diversity of subjects within a diversity of approaches to those subjects. Under the editorship of Joseph D. Lichtenberg, in collaboration with Melvin Bornstein and the editorial board of *Psychoanalytic Inquiry*, the volumes in this series strike a balance between research, theory, and clinical application. We are honored to have published the works of various innovators in psychoanalysis, including Frank Lachmann, James Fosshage, Robert Stolorow, Donna Orange, Louis Sander, Léon Wurmser, James Grotstein, Joseph Jones, Doris Brothers, Fredric Busch, and Joseph D. Lichtenberg, among others.

The series includes books and monographs on mainline psychoanalytic topics, such as sexuality, narcissism, trauma, homosexuality, jealousy, envy, and varied aspects of analytic process and technique. In our efforts to broaden the field of analytic interest, the series has incorporated and embraced innovative discoveries in infant research, self-psychology, intersubjectivity, motivational systems, affects as process, responses to cancer, borderline states, contextualism, postmodernism, attachment research and theory, medication, and mentalization. As further investigations in psychoanalysis come to fruition, we seek to present them in readable, easily comprehensible writing.

After more than 25 years, the core vision of this series remains the investigation, analysis, and discussion of developments on the cutting edge of the psychoanalytic field, inspired by a boundless spirit of inquiry. A full list of all the titles available in the *Psychoanalytic Inquiry* Book Series is available at www.routledge.com/Psychoanalytic-Inquiry-Book-Series/book-series/LEAPIBS.

The Self-Restorative Power of Music

A Psychological Perspective

Frank M. Lachmann

LONDON AND NEW YORK

First published 2022
by Routledge
2 Park Square, Milton Park, Abingdon, Oxon OX14 4RN

and by Routledge
605 Third Avenue, New York, NY 10158

Routledge is an imprint of the Taylor & Francis Group, an informa business

© 2022 Frank M. Lachmann

The right of Frank M. Lachmann to be identified as author of this work has been asserted by him in accordance with sections 77 and 78 of the Copyright, Designs and Patents Act 1988.

All rights reserved. No part of this book may be reprinted or reproduced or utilised in any form or by any electronic, mechanical, or other means, now known or hereafter invented, including photocopying and recording, or in any information storage or retrieval system, without permission in writing from the publishers.

Trademark notice: Product or corporate names may be trademarks or registered trademarks, and are used only for identification and explanation without intent to infringe.

British Library Cataloguing-in-Publication Data
A catalog record for this book is available from the British Library

Library of Congress Cataloguing-in-Publication Data
A catalog record has been requested for this book

ISBN: 978-1-032-11660-0 (hbk)
ISBN: 978-1-032-00784-7 (pbk)
ISBN: 978-1-003-22095-4 (ebk)

DOI: 10.4324/9781003220954

Typeset in Times New Roman
by Newgen Publishing UK

Contents

	Music videos	viii
	Overture	1
1	Words and melodies, psychology and music	13
2	Thrills and goose bumps in music	29
3	Music as narrative	39
4	Richard Wagner: childhood trauma and creativity	58
5	Richard Strauss: creativity in crisis and crises in creativity	75
6	Cole Porter: trauma and self-restoration	90
7	Finale: music and the Jews	105
	References	110
	Index	114

Music videos

Scan these pages of links to the music discussed in the text onto your computer. Place the YouTube page on the desktop as well. Copy the link you want to hear and paste it on the search space of the YouTube. The video that accompanies the text will appear near the top of the video list shown. Ads that often precede the videos can be deleted through a button on the lower right-hand corner of the screen. At times YouTube removes some videos and posts new ones. The reader will have to click on the video that most closely resembles the suggested one. All this sounds more complicated than it really is. Enjoy the music.

*The following links were accurate at the time of publication.

Overture

The Lambeth Walk: https://youtu.be/gWzw6gCjPng
Horst Wessel Lied Die Fahne Hoch: https://youtu.be/2mpAkNjiM-M
Kate Smith Introduces God Bless America: https://youtu.be/_zF7a0wB-Lg
Schubert Symphony # 8 The Unfinished Solti, Chicago Symphony Orchestra: https://youtu.be/1-p58OSYhG0
Grieg Peer Gynt Suite Morning Oramo Berliner Phiharmonuker: https://youtu.be/QCiQho5DzfY
The Threepenny Opera 1954 Complete at 23 minutes The Bulging Pocket: https://youtu.be/UnnkS74kGx4

Chapter 1

Chabrier—España: https://youtu.be/ZFF8l--PhHQ
Bizet Symphony in C: https://youtu.be/3TuthxWVR4U

The Merry Widow: https://youtu.be/ELufSzviGoU

Wagner Prelude and Liebestod from Tristan and Isolde: https://youtu.be/zZreeVzaOEo

Bernstein at Harvard Plays the Beethoven Sonata opus 31, #3: https://youtu.be/nezMfei5HPM

Beethoven Piano Concerto #4. Second Movement Begins at 19 minutes: https://youtu.be/e7DJMtEu4_4

Contrast a Piece of 12-tone Music by Schoenberg, Transfigured Night (https://youtu.be/3Atur0Lj3uI) with Stravinsky's The Firebird Gergiev: https://youtu.be/RZkIAVGlfWk

Chapter 2

Cole Porter Every Time Say Goodbye, Lena Horne: https://youtu.be/jqa5kNNaMlc

Schubert Piano Trio in E Flat: https://youtu.be/LFjkIrRjZZU

Sibelius Symphony No 2 op43, Bernstein Wiener Philharmoniker: https://youtu.be/SAOf46CXaaw

Shower Scene from Psycho: https://youtu.be/0WtDmbr9xyY

Chapter 3

Der Ring Des Nibelungen: Das Rheingold [Boulez]—Engl. Subs: https://youtu.be/3ZP-yXsNV2E

Renee Fleming Capricio Final Scene Engl. Subs: https://youtu.be/xnQjULW2DGo

Beethoven Symphony # 6 The Pastoral: https://youtu.be/t2VY33VXnrQ

Tchaikovsky 1812 Overture Los Angeles 2017: https://youtu.be/asUIEqA4lH4

La Marseillaise, Battle of the Bands in Casablanca: https://youtu.be/HM-E2H1ChJM

Beethoven Symphony # 9 Bernstein: https://youtu.be/IInG5nY_wrU

Bach Brandenburg Concerto # 3: https://youtu.be/QLj_gMBqHX8

x Music videos

Chapter 4

Von Weber Overture, Der Freischütz Jarajan: https://youtu.be/7ki0u NJQClI

Wagner Rienzi Overture Tennstedt, London Philharmonic: https://youtu.be/M2JjnB45D34

Wagner Overture The Flying Dutchman, Solti Cond: Copy the above words to play instead of a link

Wagner—Karajan—Tannhauser: https://youtu.be/LTyj856BtWY

Tristan und Isolde—End of Act 3—Liebestod: https://youtu.be/zZreeVzaOEo

An Introduction to Wagner's Die Meistersinger von Nürnberg: https://youtu.be/tXPY-4SMp1w

Die Meistersinger von Nürnberg subt in Italian, English. French 1995. At 1 hour and 6 minutes Walther begins his audition to become a Meistersinger so he will be eligible to marry Eva: https://youtu.be/X2ZoXZygRPw

Wagner: Die Meistersinger von Nürnberg—Akt.3.—H.Stein, Weikl, Jerusalem, Prey, Clark: https://youtu.be/qiSbrDNlPgA

Beckmesser's Humiliation at 1 hour 39 minutes

Walther's Vindication Prize Song at 1 hour 49 minutes

At 1 hour 54 minutes Walther rejects the invitation to become a Meistersinger

at 1 hour 56 minutes switch to video of conclusion with Engl. Subt.

Wagner: Die Meistersinger von Nürnburg—Finale: https://youtu.be/u61XvPYyaE0

Chapter 5

Alpine Symphony: https://youtu.be/FQhpWsRhQGs

Death and Transfiguration, Tod und Verklärung: https://youtu.be/Pd_GmPLPpRg

Don Juan: https://youtu.be/KP89c9KfetA

Symphonia Domestica: https://youtu.be/ZtOr2CblMws

Till Eulenspiegels lustige Streiche Mehta: https://youtu.be/ZU556MvQN6c

Salome Dance of the Seven Veils: https://youtu.be/hr2IiwreQ64

Salome Final Scene: https://youtu.be/cweQCnT97KI

Der Rosenkavalier: https://youtu.be/3D7abQTy71I
Overture and the Opening Scene
Nein nein ich trink ka wein 2 hours 24 minutes
Och's Exit 2 hours and 54 minutes
The most glorious trio in all opera starts at 3 hours 3 minutes
Strauss Olympic Hymn: https://youtu.be/it5O08mPQKE
Waltzes from Der Rosenkavalier Conducted by Richard Strauss: https://youtu.be/PxoP-lP8m7

Chapter 6

At Long Last Love Lena Horne: https://youtu.be/4KZbP8QhTl8

Ethel Merman and Frank Sinatra You're the Top: https://youtu.be/Vc7152gQK-U

Mary Martin My Heart Belongs to Daddy: https://youtu.be/r404p TC_qGI

Roy Rogers Sings "DON'T FENCE ME IN": https://youtu.be/WLoY FvbR0XY

Kiss Me Kate Medley, We Open in Venice: https://youtu.be/oGLlxu APcjU

Why Can't You Behave, Kiss Me Kate Why Can't You Behave
Brush Up Your Shakespeare: https://youtu.be/aSmZfnax1yw
Can Can https://youtu.be/aeM3tskWLxI

Chapter 7

David Hyde Pierce You Won't Succeed on Broadway Spamalot: https://youtube/R6VKf6bXCCo

Overture

As Jews, my parents and I had to flee from Breslau, Germany, in the Spring of 1938. We traveled to Holland, Belgium, and then to England where we boarded the *Queen Mary* for New York.

I was 8 years old, and we barely spoke English. So, a few months before we left Breslau, my parents hired an English lady, Miss Green, to come to our home to teach us all English. She had come from England to Germany, as my parents told me, because she loved Hitler.

By then, we had become accustomed to having an ardent Nazi sympathizer living in our home. In the mid-1930s, the Nazi government passed a law that Catholics were not allowed to work for Jews, but Protestants had a choice. If they wanted to continue to work for the Jews, they could. We had a Catholic nanny for me, and a Protestant maid who worked for the family. Marta, my beloved Nanny, had to leave, but Elfriede, our maid, opted to continue to work for us. However, she immediately joined the Nazi party, and faithfully attended party meetings every week. She would come back from those meetings and say very proudly, "*Unser Adolf wirds schon machen*" (Our Adolf will take care of everything). Of course, living with us, she could listen to and would report any conversations that sounded "suspicious" or critical of Hitler. We could not fire her; we had no choice but to live with her.

Furthermore, when we packed our belongings to leave Germany, Elfriede went through our apartment and pointing to paintings and furniture, with an implicit threat said, "I want this. I want that." Again, we had no choice.

The Nazi government passed another law at that time, the "Reichsfluchtsteuer." That was a tax (steuer) of 50% of the money

DOI: 10.4324/9781003220954-1

2 Overture

that you wanted to take out of Germany (Reich) because you were fleeing (flucht) from the Nazis. There was an upside to this law, however. Rather than give all that money to the Nazis, my parents booked passage on the luxurious *Queen Mary* to come to the United States. However, that law also did create a potential problem for my family because it could leave us with less money than the American Immigration Authorities required us immigrants to be able to bring to the United States in order to get a visa. To be issued a visa you had to show that you would not become a financial burden on the United States and had enough money to support your family for one year. To get around that law my parents had to get money, secretly out of Germany, before we left.

After the *Reichsfluchtsteuer* law was passed, whenever any acquaintance of my parents, usually gentile, went on a vacation or business trip to England, Belgium, or Holland, my parents would give them money to leave with a friend who lived in one of those countries. In that way we were able to get money out of Germany and eventually avoid some of the onerous tax. We would then be able to show the American Consul that we had enough money to support us for a year.

My parents' code name for money was "Dora." They would alert whoever was going to receive and hold the money for us that Dora was coming for a visit. When the money arrived, my parents would get a letter saying that Dora had arrived and was enjoying her visit. In that way, we were able to get enough money out of Germany to enable my family to get visas. To collect our Dora we went to Holland, Belgium, and England. In England we boarded the *Queen Mary* and sailed for New York.

After my parents died, when I thought about this time, I wondered how they had come up with the code name "Dora." I knew that the Nazis listened to phone conversations and censored the mail of Jews. I discovered that a law had been passed that when you spell a name in a phone conversation you were not allowed to say, "D as in David" because David was a Jewish name. You had to say, "D as in Dora." I think that made Dora a great code word.

Back to the Hitler-loving Miss Green. She taught us some expressions that she said would be useful in America. She told us that everyone in America has a favorite movie actor. And, when asked, I should say,

Overture 3

"My favorite actor is Mister Ginger Rogers." She also taught us the lyrics to a then popular English song and dance, *The Lambeth Walk*.

As luck would have it, the dance band on the British ship, *The Queen Mary*, played *The Lambeth Walk* every night. Ironically, what Miss Green had taught my parents and me turned out to provide a sorely needed sense of belonging and bridge into our new world. It weighed against our feeling that we were non-English speaking, alien misfits. Besides the British passengers on the ship, we were the only ones who could dance the Lambeth walk. It thereby restored some connection to the life we had to leave. Now let's hear *The Lambeth Walk*.

YouTube Video
The Lambeth Walk

In Germany, my father had been a lawyer. To be a lawyer in the United States required U.S. citizenship. That meant it would be at least five years before he could earn a living and that eliminated law as a profession for him. He became a Certified Public Accountant (C.P.A). That did not require citizenship, just a year of study and passing a state examination. And, thanks to Dora, we had enough money to support us for that year.

My father would do his homework for the accounting courses he took at Columbia University, and later work on the ledgers and books of his clients when he began his practice as a C.P.A., at a large handcrafted table–desk that Elfriede had not taken, and that had come with us from Germany. I would sit opposite my father on the other side of this desk to do my school homework. Behind my father, until 1941, was the Blaupunkt radio that had also come with us from Germany.

It must have been a strange experience for the Blaupunkt radio to come to New York. In Breslau, my family sat around it to learn the latest restrictions that had been imposed on the Jews. Between those news announcements it played German march music. One popular march was the *Horst Wessel Lied*. Another march, the name of which I don't remember, included the lines, "*Und wen das Judenblut durch die Strassen fliesst*" (And when the blood of Jews flows through the streets).

YouTube Video
Horst Wessel Lied

4 Overture

Only a few months later in New York, my family and I would sit around that same radio to listen to Kate Smith sing *God Bless America*, written by Irving Berlin, a Jew, no less.

YouTube Video
Kate Smith Sings God Bless America

In 1941, when World War II broke out, we had to surrender our German radio at the local New York police station. Not yet being U.S. citizens, we were considered to be German nationals and therefore enemy aliens. As such, the U.S. State Department claimed, we might get orders over short wave from Hitler and carry them out. No distinction was made between us Jews who fled from Germany and German-Americans who were members of the German-American Bundt.

We acquired a new Zenith radio which, like the Blaupunkt, was always tuned to WQXR, the classical music station in New York. For my parents, this music provided continuity and a connection to their past. For me, hearing this music served as an invitation into the life I had seen my parents live in Breslau. Since 1939, WQXR has remained my sometimes foreground, sometimes background companion. Even as I write these chapters, the classical music of WQXR accompanies me.

With music filling our home, my father and I did our respective homework. My mother and grandmother (my mother's mother, who had come with us) would be busy in the house, within earshot of the music. Music being portable and speaking an international language provided a sense of continuity with the lives my parents and my grandmother had left behind. Hearing the familiar music restored some of their socially unrestricted pre-Nazi German life in our economically restricted but socially and politically safer American life. I think that the music reminded them of who they once were, how comfortably they once lived, and thus provided a sense of continuity with that comfort. Hearing the familiar music situated them in the world that had been torn from them. Hearing music, even when only in the background, restored a sense of self that had been wrest from them and soothed the challenges of adjusting to their new life. And the music included me in their perhaps, by me, idealized but lost lives.

Growing up in Germany, I remember my parents going out at night to the opera, an operetta, the theater, or to a concert. My father would wear a tuxedo and my mother a long evening gown with a whiff of a fragrant perfume that I could smell when she kissed me goodnight. That elegant and luxurious life came to an end in the mid-1930s when Nazi storm-troopers would enter the theaters and concert halls and announce "Juden Raus" (Jews Get Out). All the Jews had to leave, in fact they would not dare stay, lest they be recognized by the gentile members of the audience who could, and would, identify and denounce them. Just from that standpoint being able to hear music in our new home in New York, without fear, built a bridge for my parents to the identities and lives that they had been forced to abandon.

Hitler became chancellor of Germany in 1933. I actually retained a memory of the day on which he was installed. I was a little more than 3 years old, and my parents and I went into the street with each of my parents holding one of my hands. What I recall is the frightening silence of the street—as though there were no people, no traffic, and therefore no sounds.

Prior to the Nazis, Germany was governed from 1919 to 1933 by a liberal government, the Weimar Republic. However, that was an unstable government right from the start. After 1918, at the end of World War I, Germany was required to pay reparations to the countries that had defeated it. However, Germany did not have the gold to pay for the reparations. The demand to pay set off political and economic crises in Germany. The Nazi party that surfaced at this time blamed the British, Americans, and the Jews for, what they considered to be, the humiliating Peace Treaty that Germany signed at Versailles. The Nazi party grew in strength, but not before Germany was plunged into a hyperinflation.

I was too young to remember this chaotic time, but my uncle Ernst, my mother's brother, kept an album of his collection of the German inflation currency, which he brought to New York. I remember seeing bills of 1000 Marks, 10,000 Marks, and even 100,000 Marks denominations. The government printed the bills to pay its debts. All were totally worthless. But there was another side to the Weimar Republic government.

During that politically and economically unsettled time, the arts, music, architecture, films, and painting flourished. And during that time, Jews did enjoy relative safety and freedom. It was a time of Jewish assimilation into German life and especially into the cultural life of Germany.

6 Overture

I know my parents had non-Jewish friends whom they invited to dinner parties and with whom they played cards. My father had non-Jewish clients. In fact, when I was about six years old one of my father's gentile clients lent us his car and chauffeur to drive us to visit my father's father who lived in a neighboring town. On the way back, I saw a man on a motorcycle come out of a side road at top speed and slammed into our car. He was badly injured and he was wearing a Nazi uniform. The police came and arrested the gentile driver of our car. My father, the lawyer, defended him in court and was able to get him freed. My memory of this event attests to the still respectful relations between Jews, non-Jews, and the German authorities. Only a short time later, the fact that the chauffeur was driving a bunch of Jews would have been used against him.

The life that my parents lost was a socially comfortable and culturally rich life that they had come to enjoy. As a lawyer, my father's clients, Jews and Gentiles, became social friends for both my parents. At their dinner parties I would be brought in to say "gute Nacht" to everybody. After dinner, the men would retire into one room, our Herrenzimmer, and the women retire into another room, our Damenzimmer. The men would play a card game called skat and smoke cigars. The women would play bridge and smoke cigarettes.

Going to the opera and concerts had been an integral part of the lives of my parents, as it was for the generation in which they grew up. A big hit in the 1930s was *Die Dreigroschenoper* (*The Threepenny Opera*) by composer Kurt Weill and librettist Berthold Brecht. The biting satire and ironic humor of the work appealed to both my parents. I did not get to see it then, but my parents would frequently quote lines from the opera, "Nur wer im Wohlstand lebt, lebt angenehm" (literally translated as "only if you live in luxury do you live comfortably"). In the English version of the opera, this line is translated as "The bulging pocket makes the easy life." (Later I will provide a link to the opera when I did get to hear it.)

As my father and I worked at our respective homework and listened to classical music, I became familiar with much of the music we heard. I developed a particular fondness for Tchaikovsky's *The Nutcracker Suite* and his *Fifth* and *Sixth Symphonies*. When these pieces, and others, were played, I would pick up a letter opener that served as a baton and interrupt my homework to conduct.

Hearing classical music playing in the background as we worked revived a connection to a familiar, secure past in contrast to our feeling like strangers in some-ways inhospitable, strange land. My schoolmates in the 3rd grade class into which I was placed welcomed me with "Go back where you came from."

In New York, my father became a college student again whereas in Germany, with his doctoral degree in law, he was called, "Herr Doktor." My mother thus was generally called "Frau Doktor." Hearing the music that they left behind served a welcomed reminder of that lost past. Listening to the music with my parents included me in that world.

Because the public schools in Breslau had been closed to Jews, I went to a Jewish school. This school had no gymnasium, so once a week we were marched through the streets of Breslau to a public gym. That was a terrifying walk for a bunch of Jewish children. After school, my friends and I would play in a park near our school under the watchful eyes of our mothers. The children of the storm-troopers had joined the Hitler Jugend, its Nazi youth division. While their fathers threw Jews out of the concert halls, their sons in the Hitler Jugend roamed the streets and parks of Breslau. Once a group of these Nazi teenagers, wearing their Hitler Jugend uniforms, surrounded us in the park and threw stones at us. Our mothers admonished us not to throw them back since that would only make matters worse. So, we scattered. The Nazi teenagers disbanded, and in a frightened state we returned to our mothers. One mother advised us to pee in the gutter of the street so we could calm down. For children to pee in the street gutter was not that unusual in Breslau. I don't remember what the girls did who were with us, but I imagine they had to calm themselves vicariously.

In thinking about that suggestion now, it seems to me that the advice was not so nutty. Although the solution had no relationship to the threat, it calmed our fright by giving us a sense that our plumbing was still intact. It was a self-restorative act that engaged our bodies. Just like music.

Music connected my parents with the world in which my father had been a successful attorney. Doing my homework as music played connected me with my parents' world and with my father, in particular, at this time.

When it came to music, I would describe my father as a conflicted Wagnerian. Wagner's anti-Semitism (about which I will have more to

8 Overture

say later) was troublesome to him. However, my father and his friends had grown up with Wagner's music. In fact, they made up scatological lyrics to some of the music from Wagner's opera, *Die Meistersinger*.

In college, I had a classmate who was an extra at performances of the Metropolitan Opera. Extras don't sing but add to the number of people in the chorus on the stage during crowd scenes. Once my friend was unable to use his pass and it happened to be for *Die Meistersinger*. He gave it to me and, although extras are not supposed to sing, I had a wonderful time singing the scatological lyrics I had learned from my father.

In addition to the operettas of Franz Lehar and Johann Strauss, which were my mother's favorites, one of my parents' favorite operas was *Der Rosenkavalier*. Through my father I had come to know and like the music of Richard Wagner and through both of my parents, the music of Richard Strauss. The music and stories of these composers occupy later chapters of this book.

When I was in 4th, 5th, and 6th grades, a citywide music appreciation program was taught in New York schools. We were required to be able to identify by name and composer about 20 compositions as soon as the opening notes were played when the teacher placed the phonograph needle on the spinning record. My parents took my assignment to learn to identify this music very seriously. So, we went to the home of my mother's cousin, Uncle John. He had brought his entire collection of 78 revolutions per minute (r.p.m.) records from Germany. Of course, he had all the recordings I had to learn to identify, and I got extra practice in identifying the music. This may not sound as the best way to get children to appreciate classical music, but it worked for me. Mnemonic devices were invented to help us recognize and remember some of the music.

To identify Schubert's *8th Symphony,* called The Unfinished, we learned to sing to its melody, "This is the symphony that Schubert wrote but never finished." And another musical helper was "This is the morning, the beautiful morning, the morning from *Peer Gynt* by Grieg."

Let's hear them.

YouTube Video
Schubert Symphony # 8 The Unfinished
Grieg Peer Gynt Suite Morning

It should come as no surprise that when I went to college, I would take a number of music courses. The high point of my college education was a course titled, "Sight singing, ear training, and conducting." I was assigned to conduct the class in singing the Steven Foster song, "In the Evening by the Moonlight." Finally, I was able to exchange the letter opener for a real baton.

My youthful fascination with conducting an orchestra was later absorbed into my interest in psychology. I think my interest in conducting was rooted in my acquaintance with the father of the first friends I made in New York. Pierre and Roger were immigrants from France and their stepfather was Maurice Abravanel. While my friends and I had our afternoon milk and cookies, Maurice would sit with us and challenge us with word games. At night he conducted the Kurt Weill musicals on Broadway. Later he became the conductor of the Utah Symphony Orchestra and one summer he became the head of the music school at Tanglewood, the summer home of the Boston Symphony Orchestra. By that time, I was an adult and owned a summer home there. One of the pleasures of living near Tanglewood is attending rehearsals of the Boston Symphony. I was able to reconnect with Maurice that summer and discovered that true to form, unlike other teachers and faculty at the music school run by the Boston Symphony, Maurice ate lunch with the students in the student's cafeteria rather than eating in the faculty dining room. He clearly wanted to offer the students as personally rich an experience as he could.

Another conductor who behaved unusually with the music students was Leonard Bernstein. When he conducted the student orchestra, he spent part of the first rehearsal connecting with many student musicians individually. He would tell the student that he remembered him or her from a previous performance, or ask someone he did not yet know to tell him more about themselves. Guest conductors only conduct a few performances with the student orchestra, but these students played for Bernstein as they did for none of the other equally renowned conductors. In music, as in psychoanalysis, the human connection carries the difference.

In its fund-raising requests, radio station WQXR in New York asserts that music is all about connections—connections between the conductor and the orchestra, the orchestra and the audience, and the

10 Overture

past and the present. The parallel to psychoanalysis is striking as we shall soon see.

My interest in psychoanalysis in relation to music came about in an unexpected way. After my first year of college, I took a summer job as a counselor in a day camp for mildly to moderately disturbed children. The camp was run by Hans Epstein, another German Jewish refugee. He was working on his doctorate degree in psychology, and as part of his course work he gave Rorschach tests to the campers. He discussed his findings at staff meetings to enable us to understand the children better. I was fascinated by what could be gleaned from the inkblots and soon began to take psychology courses. My interest in psychology had actually been stirred earlier, when for a birthday, my parents had given me a book of some of Freud's collected papers.

One evening during that summer, Hans Epstein invited the camp staff to his home to listen to some records he had just been able to obtain from Germany. It turned out to be a German recording of *Die Dreigroschenooer (The Threepenny Opera)*. What a confluence of surprising, fortuitous events. I had never heard *The Threepenny Opera* except for the lines quoted by my parents and now here it was right alongside my growing interest in psychology. Looking back, now, I think my fate was sealed. I would find in both disciplines, psychology and music, welcoming worlds that I wanted to explore and in which I wanted to live. Now, let's listen to *Die Dreigroschenoper* in its English translation by Marc Blizstein as *The Threepenny Opera*.

YouTube Video
The Threepenny Opera

This brings me to the title of my book *The Self-Restorative Power of Music*. With a tip of my hat to Descartes's dictum "I think therefore I am," I am proposing that music in all its guises, singing, listening, or playing an instrument can add affectivity to thinking and thereby makes music a powerful contributor to the "I am," that is, to the sense of self.

Singing, playing a musical instrument, and yes even listening to music can engage the whole body, not just the brain or only the vocal chords. Listening to music engaged my whole body as I picked up that letter opener to conduct. Singing, playing an instrument, and listening to music add affectivity and can restore a vulnerable sense of self which thinking may or may not be able to accomplish.

Furthermore, as Leonard Bernstein (1976), among many others, argued, music is pure emotion. As such, music has the power to transform emotions; I will illustrate throughout this book but especially in Chapter 2, *Goose-bumps*. Three chapters are devoted to composers I particularly like: Richard Wagner, Richard Strauss, and Cole Porter. I have already referred to the first two. But, as I discovered, Cole Porter turns out to be the poster boy for the self-restorative power of music as I relate later. Through the lives of all three composers, I illustrate the contributions that music can make to the sense of self, to its self-restorative, self-assertive, and authority-defying power. No doubt a similar argument can be made about many other composers. These three are not unique in this respect, but I chose them because I like their music in particular.

I can also trace my interest in the self-restorative power of music to the book on developmental arrests by Bob Stolorow and me (Stolorow and Lachmann, 1980). We proposed that the sense of self can be defined along three dimensions: temporal continuity, affective coloration, and structural cohesion.

Temporal continuity refers to the feeling that one is connected to one's past experience "I am still the same person who lived there, and at that time then, and I have also grown or changed. Time may pass but I am still me." Affective coloration refers to a general feeling of positive self-regard. The positive feeling may be shaken at some time, but at best a basic positively toned sense of self pervades. Structural cohesion means that anxiety or despair may be felt but those feelings do not take over and define the totality of one's self-experience. So far in this chapter, I have focused on the traumatic disruption of temporal continuity and how music can reinstate the sense of continuity. A sense of temporal continuity can also organize a more positively toned sense of self and a feeling of self-cohesion. Temporal continuity can counter feeling disoriented.

When my family and I came to New York, music had come to occupy a special place in our lives. I think our flight from Nazi Germany provided a background and sharp context that contributed to music being valued and given its special place. If I were to describe this transition from Germany to America musically, I would liken the contrast between life in Nazi Germany and New York to the shift from a minor key to a major key. I illustrate how that musical shift sounds and feels, later, in works by Schubert and Sibelius.

Our flight from Germany gave our enjoyment of music an extra "glow." We no longer felt so trapped and helpless. The soaring quality of some music evoked a particular feeling of joy.

In a movement from a symphony, a theme from the beginning is often reprised at the end but then appears in a new context. With that in mind, here is another reference to Elfriede. When she made her not so subtle, implicit threats, we were trapped and helpless. We had no choice but to hand over some of our furniture and valuable paintings. Her extortion really constituted a microcosm of the *Reichsfluchtsteuer*.

After World War II ended, Elfriede tracked us down in New York. She wrote to us that during the war evidence of the social security she and we had paid for her got lost. Without a word about the furniture and paintings she had forced us to give her, she asked my parents to verify that she had worked for us and that we and she paid social security for her. Now we did have a choice. God bless America.

Chapter 1

Words and melodies, psychology and music

As a young teenager, my father and I would take long walks on Saturday or Sunday afternoon. One day we walked from our home, on 79th Street in Manhattan, to about 48th street. There, to our surprise, we discovered that tickets were being distributed for a free radio concert by the American Broadcasting Company Symphony Orchestra. What an unexpected delight. We then often went to hear the A.B.C. Symphony Orchestra, conducted by Max Goberman, who was well known at that time.

The trips to hear the A.B.C. Symphony Orchestra had a special meaning to me because at these concerts my father and I often heard music that my father had not heard in Germany. This was music that both of us now heard for the first time. For example, I recall a concert at which we heard Chabrier's *España Rhapsody* and Bizet's *Symphony in C*. My father had never heard either of the works and both works soon became particular favorites.

YouTube Videos
Chabrier—España Rhapsody
Bizet Symphony in C No. i

Many years later as I was becoming a psychoanalyst and lay on my analyst's couch, associating freely, amid the memories and narratives, among the words that went through my mind, bits of music burst forth. In speaking of my relationship with my parents, I heard, in my mind's ear, a theme from Bizet's *Symphony in C*. It reminded me of the concerts I had attended with my father, at which we both heard these pieces for the first time. The music conveyed my bond with my father. In another

DOI: 10.4324/9781003220954-2

14 Words and melodies, psychology and music

hour, when recalling aspects of my relationship with my mother, I heard the waltz from Franz Lehar's operetta, *The Merry Widow*.

YouTube Video

Waltz from *The Merry Widow*

My Freudian analyst interpreted this memory as my Oedipal wish. I had gotten rid of my father in depicting my mother as a widow, which she was not, and a merry one at that. Equating the musical passage with its title did little more than substituting words for music, as though the title of the piece was my association. I think, in retrospect, it missed the point.

When my analyst interpreted my referring to *The Merry Widow* as my Oedipal wish, getting rid of my father and making merry with my mother, I recall feeling rather pleased by that interpretation. I was becoming a Freudian psychoanalyst myself at that time, so I was pleased to know that in my unconscious there lurked an Oedipus complex, just like in everyone else's unconscious, according to Freud. It gave me a feeling of belonging, not being an alien and outsider anymore.

When I subsequently thought about that interpretation, I tried to figure out what might have emerged had we investigated that musical moment rather than just interpreting the title. Other meanings might have emerged. Had we explored what *The Merry Widow* meant to me, I might have recounted that when I was about 15 years old my parents took me to see *The Merry Widow*. It was my first Broadway show. It was performed by Marta Eggert and Jan Kiepura, who had sung this operetta in German all over Europe before World War II. Now they were singing it in English, here, in New York. When my parents took me to see *The Merry Widow*, it reconnected them with an aspect of the world they had lost, and, for me, it was an invitation to enter that world with them. I was now old enough, and we could afford to go to the theater. It was a memorable moment, the kind of "heightened affective experience" about which my colleague Beatrice Beebe and I later wrote (Beebe and Lachmann, 2002, p. 134). Such experiences have an impact, an organizing influence, far beyond the actual time that they take.

The Oedipal interpretation did no harm, but it failed to acknowledge the meaning of my memory of *The Merry Widow*: a bridge to the idealized cultural and musical life that I saw my parents as having lived in Germany. It was a world and a life that I had feared would never become available to me but that I could now begin to recapture. Inadvertently, my analyst's Oedipal interpretation made me feel that I did belong to a worldwide community. As a young psychologist, I felt I was now a member of a community of people with Oedipus complexes—just like everybody else. That may not have been his intended point in making the interpretation, but I did make something of it that I needed.

The take-away is that the meanings that listeners attach to music are private, precious, and unique, a topic that I will explore further throughout this book. Had my parents taken me to hear another Johann Strauss operetta such as *Die Fledermaus* or *Zigeuner Baron*, both of which were performed in New York and both of which could have served to connect us to our European past, the meaning of the event would have been the same. Had I recalled a melody from either of these Johann Strauss operettas, I think my analyst would have had a more difficult time formulating an Oedipal interpretation out of "The Bat" or "The Gypsy Baron."

Psychology and music

Skipping over several years of my life, we now move more directly to the interface between music and psychology. To explore this connection, I turn to several essays by Heinz Kohut (1968, 1971, 1977).

I became interested in the theory of Kohut in the 1970s. In contrast to basing his theory on sexuality and aggression, as did Freud, Kohut emphasized the centrality of the sense of self. He formulated under what pressures and threats the sense of self may "fragment," relinquish a sense of cohesion, eventuating in feelings of anxiety and disorientation. Kohut then discussed how psychoanalytic treatment can lead to the restoration, transformation, and maintenance of the sense of self.

In the 1950s, before he had explicated his theory of the centrality of the sense of self, in tune with the psychological writings of his day, Kohut (1957) approached the enjoyment of music, as he did psychotherapeutic treatment and early development, from Freud's viewpoint.

"The mother's voice," wrote Kohut and Levarie (1950), "becomes associated with oral gratification for the infant; the mother's lullaby, with the drowsy satisfaction after feeding. Early kinesthetic eroticism, rocking the cradle, for example, anticipates the enjoyment of dancing and may become associated with definite rhythmic patterns" (Coriat, 1945, p. 142). Kohut was already connecting music to bodily experiences, a theme he developed further in his later writings.

The relationship between music and psychology that is contained in Kohut's writings was typical of the 1950s. It was the time when psychology relegated the arts to repressed sexual desires that push for expression as acceptable social behaviors, vicarious means of conflict resolution, and affect discharge. It was the time when psychologists promised to unveil the mysteries of the world, love, sex, and the arts. It was the time about which Leonard Bernstein (1982) said derisively, "When Dr. (Lawrence) Kubie explained the creative process by simply invoking the word *preconscious*" (p. 229).

Kohut, then adhering to a conflict resolution hypothesis, posited that listening to music presents a threat that requires mastery in that dissonance in the music and departures from the home key, create tension. When the music returns to consonance and to the home key of the composition, Kohut reasoned, there would be a sense of relief and a feeling of mastery. By referring to feelings of tension and relief, Kohut formulated listening to music as an experience that involved the whole body of the listener.

A brief excursion into musicology may help to clarify this and subsequent material. The home key, called the tonic, is the key in which a musical composition is written. The tonic defines the beginning ambience from which Western composers have developed and elaborated their musical ideas for the past 400 years.

Scales, keys, and the tones or notes that comprise them are derived from the "harmonic series," a product of the physics of sound. The harmonic series contains all notes that are heard when a plucked string (as in a violin) or a column of air (as in a flute) vibrates; that is, plucking a string stimulates other notes, called "overtones," that are in a constant relationship to each other.

The harmonic series is important because it demonstrates that tonality is an inherent physical property of vibrating objects. Different cultures, Chinese, Indian, or Western, have made up different scales by using different series of notes from the 12 tones that make up an octave.

Words and melodies, psychology and music 17

Some cultures use a five-note scale, a pentatonic scale. We use a seven-note scale, the diatonic scale. All 12 tones make a chromatic scale.

The harmonic series pulls music toward tonality. This bias was reflected in Kohut's comments, but he recognized in his later work, there is another powerful pull, a psychological pull, in analyst and analysand, and I would extend that to composer, performer, and listener. This powerful pull is the striving for self-assertion, self-articulation, and toward defining oneself uniquely. In music, these are the contrary pulls of tonality and atonality, of diatonic scales and chromatic scales, and consonant and dissonant sounds. Armed with this brief foray into Musicology 101, we turn to the relationship between the listener and the music and between music and psychology.

The model for pleasure in listening to music that Kohut utilized was Freud's theory of sexuality. It is the very theory of sexuality that he and many other psychoanalysts roundly criticized. An early critic was by George Klein (1950). But, in the 1950s, for both sexuality and music, Freud's theory dictated that the aim was to get rid of the feelings of tension, to "discharge" them, rather than to savor an exquisitely sensual total experience, including an exciting build-up of tension.

When it came to the enjoyment of sensual and sexual experiences, in pleasures of mounting tension prior to satisfaction through a feeling of release, or orgasm, poets, lovers, and composers had been way ahead of the psychologists. The artists and lovers all saw foreplay, the romantic build-up of excitement and tension as an inextricable part of the pleasurable sexual arousal.

An excellent example of elongating foreplay is Richard Wagner stretching the erotic yearning of Tristan and Isolde for each other over four hours. Wagner does so through a series of excruciatingly ambiguous chord progressions that do not resolve but rather lead to another unresolved chord. That is how the *Prelude* begins the opera, and the unresolved chords only reach a musical resolution at the very end of the opera. They are excruciating because each unresolved chord in this *Prelude*, in which a key is not clearly indicated, does not come to a resolution until the very last notes of the opera, in Tristan and Isolde's love-death. There the chord progressions are resolved, indicating that the two lovers have finally consummated their erotic desires after death. We will encounter Tristan and Isolde again in the chapter

18 Words and melodies, psychology and music

on Wagner, but here is a preview of the orchestral version, without voices.

YouTube Video
Wagner Prelude and Liebestod
from *Tristan and Isolde*

Like foreplay in sex, *departures* from consonance and the tonic key provide pleasure. They do so not *only* because of the expected return home, although such an expectation may be in the background, but the very violations of the departures are pleasurable.

Departures from the tonic, excursions through modulations in different keys, and violations of expectations are characteristic of the development sections of musical compositions. In symphonic music, for example, themes are taken up by different instruments and played in different keys. In effect, they are "worked through." Like analyst and analysand, the performer and listener find a new way of looking at and hearing old material. The old material appears in an ever-changing context. As in psychological therapy, in music, working through is not designed to eliminate the impact of the old, but rather to embed it in a variety of new contexts. Thereby the old is given a richer texture in the present. In both psychological treatment and in listening to music, active creative participation is required by all participants, performers, and listeners.

In writing about music, Heinz Kohut also *departed* from his traditional psychological perspective and hinted at novel interfaces between music and psychology. First, Kohut (1957) linked the function of music to the function of the psychotherapist. He extrapolated from Freud's advice about listening to patients with evenly hovering attention by recommending that therapists should listen to "the sounds of the patient's voice, the music that lies behind the meaningful words" (p. 243). In listening to a patient's music, and not only the words, Kohut paved the way, but was not yet ready to include the therapist's music, the therapist's empathic immersion as a co-creator in the patient's experience. He was not yet ready to depict psychotherapeutic treatment as an improvisational duet.

Second, Kohut (1957) recognized the central role of repetitions and rhythm in musical compositions. However, he related the prevalence and acceptance of repetitions in music to a reduction in energy expenditure. He did not yet have access to the empirical infant research which demonstrated that rhythms can forge powerful connections (Jaffe, Beebe, Feldstein, Crown, and Jasnow, 2001).

Third, Kohut likened music to "play," thereby departing from the anxiety-tension-reduction model of musical enjoyment. However, he linked the enjoyment of music to Freud's observations of a child playing "being gone" in order to master actively the painful passively endured experience of its mother's absence.

Fourth, Kohut compared music and poetry. A simple rhythm may be covered or concealed by a sophisticated tune just like the deeper primary-process layer of rhythm or rhyme may be covered by the verbal content of a poem. Here Kohut pointed toward a broader, more complex artistic organization comprising surface structures and deeper structures. This parallel between poetry and music also fascinated Leonard Bernstein as discussed below.

At the time Kohut wrote that the pleasures of music are rooted in early oral gratification, another psychoanalyst, Ralph Greenson (1954, Lachmann, 2014a) theorized, in a similar vein, in his paper, "On the Meaning of the Sound 'Mm'" as in a then popular ad for Campbell Soup:

> Mmm, Mmm, Good,
> Mmm, Mmm, Good,
> That's what Campbell's Soups are,
> Mmm, Mmm, Good.

Greenson speculated that this sound, "Mmm," made with closed lips, is the only sound a nursing baby can make and still keep all the milk in his mouth. Greenson supported his view by listing all the languages in which the word *mother* begins with or builds on the "Mmm" sound: mama, mommy, mutter, madre, mere, and so on.

Fast forward to the 1970s. Although Greenson did not pursue the evolution of the Mmm sound and Kohut never updated his study of music in accord to his later self-psychology contributions, Leonard Bernstein took up both of these challenges. He presented his ideas in his Norton Lecture series, given at Harvard in 1976, titled, "The Unanswered Question," utilizing the title of the composition by Charles

Ives. This question is, "Whither Music?" Remarkably, Bernstein's ideas are quite consistent with Kohut's theories, especially as informed by contributions from empirical infant research.

Bernstein (1976) credited two major sources that influence his ideas. One source was the work of linguist, philosopher, and cognitive researcher Noam Chomsky on the deep structures of grammar, transformational grammar. Bernstein wanted to parallel Chomsky's work by delineating comparable deep structures, transformational processes, for music. Bernstein was also influenced by his Harvard Philosophy Professor David Presall's cross-disciplinary emphasis: the best way to know one discipline is in the context of another discipline. So, Bernstein set out to examine the structure of music in the context of poetry, linguistics, aesthetics, and physics.

One night in 1973, Leonard Bernstein (1976) said, he could not sleep and he spent the night speculating about the origins of music. His musings were similar to Greenson's but with a twist. For Greenson the sound *Mmm* was linked to oral gratification. Bernstein, however, linked what he imagined to be primal *Mmm* and *Aaa* sounds to the foundation of music and to communication.

Bernstein imagined a newborn in prehistoric times trying out his newfound voice, *Mmm*, just like Greenson's baby. However, when hungry, Bernstein imagined an infant calling for his mother's attention with *Mmm, Mmm*, and opening his mouth to receive the nipple, *Mmm-Aaa*. Then with an intensification of hunger or with impatience or delight, the word is prolonged, *Maaa*. And, imagined Bernstein, from his evolutionary perspective, we are now singing. "What we seem to be getting to," he wrote, "is a hypothesis that would confirm a cliché—namely, Music is Heightened Speech" (p. 15). The cause of such heightening would be intensified emotion. However, in the remainder of the lectures, Bernstein challenged that cliché. Music is even more, much more, than heightened speech.

For Greenson and Kohut, their infant made sounds, and satisfactions or rewards reinforced these sounds. Bernstein's infant, however, anticipated the motivational systems theory of Joe Lichtenberg, Jim Fosshage, and Lachmann (2010). Bernstein's infant was motivated by sensuality, needs to exercise physiological functions and to meet physiological requirements, and was motivated by curiosity, exploration,

Words and melodies, psychology and music   21

assertion, and attachment. Thus, following Bernstein, music, communication, motivational systems theory, and infant research all share a common beginning in prehistoric times.

These speculations, however, do not yet include a responsive environment whereby infant and caregiver co-construct and interactively regulate experiences of satisfaction and frustration. The infant is still depicted as essentially shaped by, but not yet shaping, its environment. Yet Bernstein did recognize a co-construction model in the creation of the musical experience, as he demonstrated in his lectures.

Listening to music is, of course, complexly embedded in cultural, emotional, intellectual, and developmental influences. It becomes an interactive process, in which we can be piqued by curiosity, delighted by novelty, enticed by the unexpected, and shocked by surprises. Pleasure resides in the challenge as we follow the intricacies of the music. We crescendo with joy and decrescendo in exhaustion. But, most important, we have to engage in a manner that co-constructs the musical experience with the composer and performer.

As in the empirical infant research, in listening to music, co-construction does not mean that each participant, composer, performer, and listener contributes similarly or equally to the experience. Rather, each contributes, influences, and is influenced by the other in some manner. When Bernstein plays the Beethoven Sonata opus 31, #3, for example, he feels the notes as longings and teasing. He "hears" and plays a dialogue between the plaintive opening bars and the somewhat sterner melodic response. Through his performance, he illustrates the co-construction of the musical experience by composer, performer, and listener. But from where do these yearnings arise, these feelings that Bernstein expresses as he plays? Is it in the music? Is it in Bernstein as performer? Or Bernstein as listener? Is it intrinsic to the "meaning" of the music?

YouTube Video
Bernstein Plays Beethoven Sonata opus 31, #3

Bernstein (1976) asked, "Did Beethoven feel all that, or anything like it? Did I make up these feelings, or are they to some degree related to Beethoven's feelings transferred to me through his notes?" (p. 138).

22 Words and melodies, psychology and music

His response is "both" and is consistent with his belief in the inherent ambiguity of music and the power of expressivity of music.

Bernstein distinguished the expressive power of music from the meaning of music. Expressive power relies on the contributions of the listener as in the just discussed Beethoven Piano Sonata. Musical meanings are different, Bernstein emphasized. Music does not mean anything literal. It is abstract, generated by a constant stream of metaphors and transformations. But, I argue, as listeners, we do endow music with personal meaning as I have illustrated so far, with the Bizet *Symphony in C* and *The Merry Widow*.

Like Kohut, Bernstein draws a parallel between poetry and music. He argues that prose can be transformed into poetry through metaphors and various figures of speech, for example, deletions and devices such as embedding, thesis and antithesis, and repetition.

Here is some prose: Juliet is a girl. Romeo's usual temperature is 98.6 degrees Fahrenheit. When Romeo stands near Juliet, his temperature rises to 98.8 degrees Fahrenheit. The sun is at the center of our solar system. The rays of the sun light up and warm those parts of the earth that they touch. Here is Shakespeare's poetic version of that prose: "Juliet is the sun." Considerable deletions of the prose are required to create the poetic metaphor "Juliet is the sun."

In music, transformations are accomplished through "figures of speech" and similar devices: thesis and antithesis, opposition of consonance and dissonance, imitation, alliteration, varieties of rhythms, harmonic progressions, symmetry, and repetitions. Symmetry and repetition occupy a special place. When we listen to music, we are primed to expect balance, symmetry, and repetition. Violations of expectations and violations of symmetry become the source of excitement that music evokes.

June Hadley (1989), a neurobiologist, found that, primarily, we are neurologically programmed to seek repetition and the novel, then to maintain arousal within tolerable limits, and then to seek pleasure and to avoid pain. Just as in early development, violations of expectations of the familiar, within certain limits, are attention grabbers. They rivet our interest and delight us. As listeners to music, we expect the familiar and the novel. As did Leonard Bernstein when he played the Beethoven Sonata, we also impose our own shape on what we hear. Together with the performer, live or recorded, we co-construct a personal and highly abstract aesthetic experience.

Repetition in music introduces a sense of time, in some ways real time. Like the ticking of a clock, repetition contains, moves, and frames the listening experience. Philosopher Susan Langer (1953) explained that "the ticking of a clock is repetitious and regular, but not in itself rhythmic; the listener's ear hears rhythm in the succession of equal ticks" (p. 126). With Dan Stern (1995), she holds that rhythm is our subjective way of organizing repeating units of time. We move with rhythm, and rhythm makes us, and music, move. Our experience of repetition is derived from our capacity, already present at birth, to distinguish rhythms. According to infant researchers DeCasper and Carstens (1980), rhythm discrimination does not need to be learned. Stern (1995) placed repetitions and rhythm, a beat that repeats, at a critical juncture in the construction of representations and in the temporal contouring of feelings. Rhythms can be a source of familiarity and novelty, as well as the scaffold for affect.

Empirical studies of the extraordinary place of rhythm have yielded a voluminous literature on vocal rhythm coordination between adult pairs and between infants and adults.

In vocal rhythm coordination (Jaffe et al., 2001), microphones are placed on the neck of each member of the two conversationalists being studied. The microphones do not pick up the content of the dialogue; rather they pick up the on–off pattern of sound and silence. That is, they pick up the rhythm of the speaker but not the words. They track variables such as vocalization, pausing, and the patterns of turn taking, how partners in a conversation negotiate when one talks and then stops talking and the other begins to talk. Vocal rhythm coordination means that each person's rhythm is predictable from that of the other. Adult partners in a conversation tend to coordinate with each other's vocal rhythm. Adults have two modes of speaking—adult-directed speech and infant-directed speech. Infants have only one mode. When adults speak with infants, they alter their pitch, rhythm, and usual manner of speech. Although they talk in "infanteze," a rhythm of turn taking is nevertheless established.

Vocal rhythm in speech is a basic ingredient of interactions and it predicts secure attachments between the two participants. Vocal

24 Words and melodies, psychology and music

rhythms are interactively organized. Greenson and Bernstein could have imagined mother–infant pairs in which the infants *Mm* to their mothers and the mothers make sounds that approximate the baby's vocalization; thereby the verbal–musical repertoire of the babies can increase. Similarly, as we listen to music or to the associations of our patients, our accompanying rhythms are likely to alter, as we mold our rhythms to the rhythms of the other and they mold their rhythms to ours. In this rhythmic interaction, our own repertoire of rhythms will increase. The beat of our music and that of our patients can be coordinated or syncopated, but, one hopes, we do not get too far off the beat.

Coordinating one's own vocal timing with that of the partner, whether infant or adult, is crucial for the infant's social development, as well as for adult relationships. This molding or coordination occurs outside of awareness. It belongs to the realm of procedural memory, to skills or action sequences that are encoded as procedures. An example of procedural memory might be how to drive a car after you have learned to drive and have driven for a while. Over time, these procedures become automatic and influence processes that guide behavior. In adults, procedural memories are content-free, in the sense that they entail the learning of processes rather than information. Procedural memories guide the way in which we engage in a dialogue.

When jazz musicians improvise, they converse with each other and with their listeners. People talking; musicians improvising; soloists, duos, or soloist and an orchestra playing are all engaged in dialogues. The dialogue may be abstract and ambiguous, but some degree of turn-taking still prevails. Compare an infant–adult "conversation," which already has the structure of two people talking but may consist only of giggles and sounds, with the dialogue between the piano and the strings from Beethoven's Piano Concerto #4.

In his *Piano Concerto in G # 4* Beethoven offers an illustration of a dialogue without the use of words, just through music. The second movement of this concerto begins as a conversation between the strings and the piano. The string instruments make an assertive statement, and the piano responds in a more placating tone. They go back and forth a few times until they finally get together.

YouTube Video
Beethoven Piano Concerto #4 2nd mvt.

Words and melodies, psychology and music 25

We are born with an orientation toward rhythmically coordinated interpersonal interactions, a sharing of our pulses and our heartbeats. In fact, Bach scholar Russell Miles (Lachmann, 1950) proposed, the beat of Baroque music, the beat of Bach's music, was the beat of the human heart, about 72 beats per minute. The conductor needs to maintain a steady beat. According to Miles, when Bach wanted the music to move more slowly, he would write it in half or whole notes. When Bach wanted the music to move more rapidly, he would write it in eighth and sixteenth notes. The harmonic series is derived from physics, but rhythms are derived from the biology and physiology of the body.

Rhythm and time, the regularity of beats, and the spacing of beats into a time frame are basic organizations that hold together dialogues between infant and caretaker, between conversationalists, and between musician and listener.

The evolution of music from its origins in *Mmm, Aaah,* and *Ma* to the time of Bach took many centuries. However, coexisting with all the transformations that characterized musical history, tonality retained its hold. After all, as Leonard Bernstein has argued, it derived from a fundamental physical principle, a universal. Tonality began to be undermined in 19th-century music. It crumbled in the beginning of the 20th century. The door to the challenge of musical tradition was opened by the operas of Richard Wagner and later the impressionistic works of Claude Debussy. In different ways for each, chromaticism gained the upper hand over diatonism. Recall the unsettling opening chords of *Tristan and Isolde.* Nevertheless, both Wagner and Debussy still retained a hold on form. In spite of their tonal revolutions and their studied ambiguities, their compositions retained an impeccable structure. But the die was cast, and in the early 20th century, composers made concerted efforts to break the mold of tonal music. Foremost among these renegades was Arnold Schoenberg. He devised a system of music called Twelve Tone; no note could be repeated until all the other 11 notes had been used. Theodor Adorno in "The Philosophy of Modern Music" (as cited in Bernstein, 1976) passionately defended Schoenberg, considering his work totally sincere, all truth and beauty, as opposed to what he considered to be the epitome of insincere music, Igor Stravinsky. Yet, though admiring of Schoenberg, Bernstein (1976) weighed in on the side of Stravinsky. He summed it up as follows:

26 Words and melodies, psychology and music

Stravinsky and Schoenberg were after the same thing in different ways. Stravinsky tried to keep musical progress on the move by driving tonal and structural ambiguities on and on to a point of no return.

Schoenberg, foreseeing this point of no return, and taking his cue from the Expressionist movement in the other arts, initiated a clean, total break with tonality altogether, as well as with symmetry.

(p. 271)

The point of no return is the point at which there is no more tonality, no more home key, and a break with the past. It is a point toward which Stravinsky moved, but never reached. Yet even in 12-tone music there is organization of sorts but not the anchor provided by tonality. Bernstein's Norton Lectures were a plea for a measure of tonality. His argument resembled Kohut's (1981) reference to the astronauts in orbit. At a possible point of no return for them, they voiced a preference for crashing into the earth, returning home, rather than spinning off into space. Similarly, Bernstein is arguing for a return to the home key.

Adorno's arguments have a familiar ring to followers of the controversies in the psychology literature. Adorno described Schoenberg's music as sincere and authentic, whereas Stravinsky's music was insincere and inauthentic. Schoenberg's work was stark, quite ingenious, deeply personal, and subjective. Stravinsky's work was detached, objective, and regressive, which meant that he maintained a connection with the past. However, to some listeners Schoenberg sounds mechanical and Stravinsky sounds serious, yet with humor, irony, and whimsy. My preference, given a choice between these two composers, is for Stravinsky. Try this experiment.

Play on YouTube Video the 12-tone music by Schoenberg
Transfigured Night
and contrast it to Stravinsky's *The Firebird*

The survival of music, in the face of renegades and fads, following Bernstein, is based on the recognition and acceptance of certain "universals." Tonality is deeply rooted in us. It is like a container.

It provides continuity and a "fence" around musical excursions, variations, adventures, and experiments. We are bound to tonality and rhythm, not only by conventions, traditions, and education, but by the universal of the harmonic series and our bearing hearts.

Let us position psychology, psychotherapy, and psychoanalysis in the realm of the arts, (Lachmann, 2016) of poetry and music, an area defined by ambiguity and abstraction. In psychological discourse, as in music, there is an ambiguity where the meanings of one participant or contributor overlap with the meanings of another. These are our procedures, where our rhythms and communications interface.

Like Kohut (1981) in his description of the astronauts who preferred to die by crashing into the earth, going home, rather than spinning off endlessly into space, if it came down to it, Bernstein envisioned the rediscovery and reacceptance of tonality in the latter part of the 20th century as furthering musical progress in "friendly competition." Like Kohut, Bernstein envisioned intergenerational mentoring as triumphing over competitive rivalries. Progress in music is built on two interconnected universals: the harmonic series assuring the survival of tonality and a musical syntax, which, like poetry, utilizes metaphors and recognizes the appeal of symmetry and repetition as well as violations of expectations. This was Bernstein's answer to the question, "Whither music?"

And "Whither psychology, psychotherapy, and psychoanalysis?" Universals tend to give us indigestion. We don't trust them because we value the infinite variety of human nature. But let us consider psychotherapeutic treatment as an art form like poetry and music, not a branch of philosophy, not a branch of a natural or even humanistic science, not a branch of biology or physics, but as an art. Psychotherapeutic treatment may share some perspectives with philosophy and science but grows out of our shared rhythms of communication. Therapist and patient are both performers and listeners, co-composing a therapeutic interlude to celebrate the unique individuality we prize: our dissonant natures, our chromatic emotions, and our atonal self-states. In those improvisational duet, faint voices get amplified, and blaring, strident voices get muted, inner voices become themes, and themes modulate into other themes. Rhythms are shared and syncopated. Music emerges, previously unheard by either participant.

Like psychotherapists, as we listen to music, we are far more actively engaged than had been previously recognized. Rather than *reducing* music to a psychological function, such as tension relief or heightened speech, we can raise psychotherapy to that ambiguous, abstract realm alongside music, where it will not wither. With a grip on our tonality, we can again proclaim: I sing; therefore, I am.

Chapter 2

Thrills and goose bumps in music

There is some controversy whether we should accept Descartes's dictum as stated, "I think therefore I am" or reverse it: "I am therefore I think." However, I believe, both are true and reciprocal, each one reinforces the other. This is particularly true when it comes to one's relationship to music, either by singing, listening to music, or playing an instrument. In those circumstances, the power of music to restore or affirm the sense of self is most evident. Hence, in illustrating that the power of music can restore the sense of self, I am placing more emphasis on "I sing therefore I am."

Music, whether by listening, singing, or playing an instrument, engages the whole body and affect. Benjamin Franklin contributed to this dialogue when he allegedly said, "Tell me and I'll listen. Teach me and I'll learn. Engage me and I'll remember." Engaging others constitutes an emotional connection. Whether as teachers, therapists, lecturers, musicians, actors, dancers, lawyers, doctors, or in business, whether speaking with one other person, a small group, or to a large audience, our aims are similar: to feel moved and to engage and move others emotionally. But first, one caveat. I use the terms affects, feelings, and emotions interchangeably. I know there is a whole literature on the distinctions among these terms but, bear with me while I ignore it.

The process of emotional engagement, according to evolutionary biologists, is closely linked to how we communicate with each other. And we engage and communicate with each other through sounds, actions, and words. Although language is important, affect is central to engagement. In fact, unless our words strike an emotional chord, they will feel flat. That's when we, or others, sound boring and we feel bored and disconnected from the speaker.

DOI: 10.4324/9781003220954-3

30 Thrills and goose bumps in music

I focus on two routes to striking an emotional chord, to emotional engagement. One route is direct and that is through music. Music, as I have just argued, engages emotions directly, and it does so without meaning or language although a listener will ascribe meaning or a narrative to it, as I illustrated in Chapter 1.

A second route to emotional engagement is based on meeting, surpassing, but especially through violating expectations. When a basic expectation of living in an emotionally responsive, predictable world is met, we feel relatively safe. When our expectations are surpassed, for example, when we fall in love and it is reciprocated, we are in heaven. When our expectations are violated and that can range from, for example, someone throwing us a surprise party, winning an unexpected award, to being mugged in the street. In these instances, strong emotions are invariably aroused. They can range from pleasure to embarrassment and to fright. These two routes to emotional engagement and change—music and meeting, surpassing or violating expectations—are sometimes connected. And in one particular instance, when they are connected, we experience goose bumps.

Music directly transforms affect; it transforms the emotional state of those who perform the music as well as those who listen to it. What a listener brings to the music listening process, such as words and meanings, language, cognition, and symbolization, can contribute to a music-listening experience, and even enhance it. But, it is the music itself that can directly evoke affect with or without words. Recall that my "hearing" in my mind, the Bizet Symphony in C evoked feelings for my father, without any words.

Steven Mithens (2006) added science to Leonard Bernstein's (1976) speculation about music and communication as described in the previous chapter. Mithens wrote, from an evolutionary standpoint, that music and language shared a common prehistoric origin. He argued that music, varying one's sounds tonally, once provided the underlying glue for human communication as far back as Neanderthal times. Like Bernstein, Mithens also considers music to be the language of emotions.

Jaak Panksepp, a neuroscientist, and Colwyn Trevarthen, an infant researcher (2009), stated in their exhaustive study of the neuroscience of emotion in music, "Music is the 'language' of emotions, and its affective power arises from subcortical emotional systems" (p. 132). In

Thrills and goose bumps in music   31

his research, Jaak Panksepp (1998) identified a specific aspect of music that triggers powerful affects and he linked this trigger to mother–infant communication. He studied the separation–distress–vocalizations made by young animals when they strayed away from their mothers and from their homes. Panksepp argued that the mother's response to her infant's distress vocalizations, as well as the quality of the distress signal, constitutes part of our evolutionary heritage. This heritage acts like a tuning fork in our bodies. When we hear certain sounds, sounds that to the listener constitutes a violation of expectations, the whole body may tingle. Those are the goose bumps we feel.

Separation–distress–vocalization refers to a cry made by baby animals, like the baby rats that Panksepp studied. Baby rats are born quite mobile and thus will wander off, away from their mothers, shortly after birth. When they do so and find themselves alone, they make a cry of distress. Human neonates, however, cannot easily wander off so they do not exhibit separation–distress–vocalizations until about 7–10 months of age. Then they have matured sufficiently to crawl off, feel lost, or at least their mother is out of sight. They then make sad and sometimes angry sounds of protest to attract the attention of their mothers.

Separation–distress–vocalizations are a kind of longing cry and the response of the mother, whether rat or human, upon hearing it, is to seek a reunion with her baby. The proximity of the mother is usually enough to quell the distress calls. Furthermore, according to Panksepp, "the neural system for separation-induced crying emerged from more primitive distress mechanisms, such as those that mediate pain and feelings of coldness," a chill (Panksepp, 1998, p. 266). Panksepp found that the cry of the baby animal evokes a cold feeling, a chill, in the mother and through her reunion behavior the two bodies, mother and baby, come into close proximity. That literally creates warmth in both partners.

The sequence is: baby wanders away, is separated from a secure base, vocalizes a distress cry, and the distress cry evokes a "chill," an experience of coldness in the mother. Those are the goose bumps. The warmth of the contact calms the infant and reregulates the thermal disequilibrium of the mother. This constitutes a loss–longing–reunion sequence, laid down by evolution. Now comes a speculation: Can this be the evolutionary basis for our hugging each other?

32 Thrills and goose bumps in music

We humans not only experience a chill in response to a soul pier-cing cry from a lost or helpless infant, but under another circumstance, chills or goose bumps are reported by many people at specific moments when they hear certain music. Panksepp (1998) speculated that

> transient arousal of our ancient separation distress response system (can be) felt during certain aesthetic experiences. (And) ... one of the most intriguing manifestations of separation distress in the human brain may reflect a powerful response many of us have to certain types of music. (Music) is one of the few ways that humans can allow the external world voluntary access to their emotional systems on a very regular basis. A common experience that people report when listening to sad songs—especially bitter-sweet songs of unrequited love and loss—melancholy songs of lost love and longing, ... is a shiver up and down the spine, which often spreads down the arms and legs, and, indeed, all over the body.
>
> (p. 278)

Panksepp refers to this as a musical chill.

Music offers a direct route to our autonomic nervous system and to an evolutionary laid-down emotional response. Panksepp called this response a musical chill because the bodily reaction reflects a "local skin contraction ... caused by evaporative cooling of the skin's sur-face" (p. 278). These are the goose bumps that are a manifestation of the emotions, the longings that have been stirred. The goose bumps are evidence that we are responding automatically, autonomically, and emotionally. Women listening to music tended to label this reaction "chills," but men described it as "thrills." Because women report this experience more frequently that do men, Panksepp (1995) went with the "chills" designation.

Panksepp proposed that acoustically sad music resembles separation–distress–vocalizations—the primal cry of being lost or in despair. The poignant feelings that are evoked by these sounds are based on our evolutionary heritage. Physiologically, we respond to certain music as though it was a separation–distress signal.

In music,

> a high-pitched sustained crescendo capable of piercing the "soul" seems to be an ideal stimulus for evoking chills. The chills we

experience during music may represent the natural tendency of our brain's emotional systems ... to react with an appropriate homeostatic thermal response, nature's way of promoting reunion.

(p. 278)

In other words, when we hear certain music, our brain and body react with a response laid down by evolution. We react as though we are the mother whose baby has just crawled off and we are alarmed by its disappearance and its cry for help. Our response is that our body temperature drops a bit. That is when we feel goose bumps or musical chills.

Panksepp's work has led to investigations of the phenomenon of musical chills. Crewe, Nagel, Kopiez, and Altenmueller (2007) found that the chill response is not tied to any specific musical style but is reported by listeners to a variety of musical styles, including Bach, Hip Hop, Rock and Roll, and to vocal and instrumental music as well.

The participants in their research, college student volunteers, were asked to bring their own recordings of music they liked. They were not informed that "chills" would be studied. As they listened to the music as part of the study, they were instructed to indicate if and when they felt a "chill." The frequency of chill experiences was found to be greater when listening to music with which the listener was familiar than if the musical style was not familiar. Here responses of a student to their own music were compared to the responses of listening to recordings brought by other students. Further investigation led the researchers to conclude that the chill response usually occurred in the familiar piece when something new or unexpected occurred, such as an unexpected harmony or a sudden dynamic or textural change. That is, the music that evokes a chill can only sound "unexpected" if it occurs in a context that is already familiar to the listener. I will soon discuss the apparent contradiction: if something unexpected gets repeated how can it remain "unexpected?"

In teasing apart the process by which chills are evoked, the researchers proposed that, to begin with, there must be a "violation of an expectation" (p. 312) in the listener, such as the beginning of something new, an entry of a voice, or a crescendo, for example, the high notes sung by sopranos, as in an illustration to which I refer in Chapter 5, the final scene from Richard Strauss's *Der Rosenkavalier* in which two sopranos and a mezzo-soprano blend their voices and rise above each other.

Flutes or piccolos against a violin tremolo background or a shift in key from minor to major are also frequently noted musical event that evoked chills.

Cole Porter refers to such a shift, but from major to minor, literally, in the lyrics to his song, "Every time we say goodbye I cry a little."

YouTube Video
Cole Porter Every Time We Say Goodbye

The shift in the other direction, from minor key to major key, usually shifts the listener from a sad mood, filled with yearning and longing, to a sudden bright "reunion-like" possibility. This shift will be illustrated later in the ending of Sibelius's Symphony #2. The shift to the major key then feels thrilling. Put differently, the composer set-up a sad, yearning, longing experience in the listener. This set-up is then violated. The shift in the music from yearning or separation distress to reunion serves as a violation of what the listener had been led to, or had come to, expect. An expectation had been set-up and violated and the listener feels goose bumps.

I was intrigued by Crewe and his co-workers' (2007, 2009) use of the concept, violations of expectations—a topic from infant research about which I have also written (Lachmann, 2008). These researchers came upon the role of expectations and their violation through a different avenue from the one I followed. My point is that a prerequisite for the experience of chills is an expectation of the familiar, a sense of being in familiar, safe, or predictable surroundings. Goose bumps are a consequence not only of how those expectations are violated, as in the high-pitched tremolos, but also that established expectations have been violated.

I have been describing the goose bump experience primarily from the side of the mother, listener, and the audience. What is it like for a performer? World-famous cellist, Yo-Yo Ma, to the rescue. In discussing his playing of a melody that recurs several times in the Schubert sonata in Eb for piano, violin, and cello. Yo-Yo Ma (Bulluck, 2011) explained that he has to set up the final repetition of the melody just right, so that it sounds as though the sun comes out. It's like you've been under a cloud and you are looking once again at a vista and then the light is shining on the whole valley. ... It's a deviation from a pattern. A surprise is only a surprise when you know it departs from something. It goes from a march theme that is in a minor and it breaks out into a major.

And then Ma adds, "it's one of those goose-bump moments" (p. D4).

YouTube Video
Schubert Piano Trio in E Flat Major

My introduction to the phenomenon of goose bumps in music occurred through reading Alex Ross's (2007) fascinating book *The Rest Noise*. In his chapter on Shostakovich, specifically his *Fifth Symphony*, Ross said that he had a chill upon hearing the Third Movement of that work. I listened to the Shostakovich symphony and the third movement, but I felt nothing, no chill. Probably I was not familiar enough with this work to have expectations that could be violated. But I do have shivers listening to the finale of Sibelius's *Second Symphony*. Somewhat similar to Schubert, Sibelius repeats his theme in a minor key over and over. You really get to know it and anticipate it. It evokes a dreary, lonesome, barren sun-less Finnish countryside. But then, suddenly, the theme turns from minor to major. As Yo-Yo Ma said about the Schubert trio, it also feels like the sun suddenly breaks through the dark clouds. And, as I have speculated, the repeated minor theme evokes a feeling of yearning and longing. Its transformation into a major key, a violation of expectations, feels like the longed-for reunion experience. As you watch this video, note that Bernstein lets you know when this shift occurs by jumping into the air as he conducts.

YouTube Video
Sibelius Symphony No 2 in D Major Op 43, 4th Movement.
Bernstein Wiener Philharmonike

Violations of expectations make a necessary, but not sufficient, contribution to the effectiveness of the chill response. A quick look at the Singer and Fagen (1992) study where 4-month-old infants had one foot tied to a mobile. The babies enjoyed kicking their foot and thereby

36 Thrills and goose bumps in music

making the mobile move. In the second phase of the study when the babies kicked, nothing happened. The ribbon had been disconnected from the baby's leg, so the mobile did not move. An expectation had been established and the babies had experienced a sense of agency. And then their expectations were violated.

As expectations become established, breaches or violations of expectations exercise a powerful organizing effect whether the breach comes from environmental circumstances or through social interactions. These studies as well as a host of others have led researchers Haith, Hazan, and Goodman (1988) to propose that infants have an innate motivation to detect patterns and contingent relations and generate procedural expectancies of the occurrence of events. Although there are many variations of expectations, core expectations, as I have suggested, are of living in a predictable world as well as expectations of affective responsivity from caretakers. Some life experiences may meet these expectations, some may pleasurably surpass them, and some, for better or worse, may violate them. Because it was violations of expectations that were linked to the goose bump phenomenon, I will continue to focus predominantly on violations of expectations.

An illustration follows in which you may have the experience of having your expectations violated, a violation of expectations evoking terror. I am referring to the well-known shower scene from Alfred Hitchcock's movie, *Psycho*. It graphically illustrates violations of expectations at their most terrifying.

Recall that we are brought into the familiar, safe, mundane world of the bathroom shower. We are led to expect that we can relax, unwind, and wash away the cares of the day. The setting establishes an expectation in Janet Leigh as well as in us, the audience, that we are living in a familiar, predictable world. Perhaps the worst thing that can happen is that the shower drain can be a bit slow, or the hot water turns cold when someone in our vicinity turns on their shower. Then an unbelievably shocking violation of our expectations intrudes. Our world and our expectations, as members of the audience, are violated. Also note that ironically, and perhaps intuitively, Bernard Herrmann's music resembles the screech of an animal in pain, a distress vocalization if there ever was one.

YouTube Video
Shower Scene from Psycho

Although we are sitting safely in a theater or in another place of comfort, when watching this scene, our breathing changes and we feel some form of fear, aversion, disbelief, even if we have seen it before. Nevertheless, we were lulled into dropping our guard, and became emotionally engaged. Our expectation and trust in the safety and predictability of our surroundings was violated. If I were to pursue this path, which I won't at this time, we would be discussing the role of violations of expectations in trauma.

This film scene illustrates violations of expectations in the characters as well as in us, the audience. And now I return to a point I dropped earlier. Having seen this clip innumerable times, the question arises: Once you have had your expectations violated in a piece of music or as in the scene from *Psycho*, wouldn't the next time you encounter this experience be "familiar" and not be so shocking? How often can I get a chill from Sibelius's music or be shocked by the movie scene? My answer is "every time!"

Why, after a number of exposures, doesn't the violation become the *expected*, rather than remain a surprise or shock? Why doesn't the repeated experience of hearing the musical event that evokes a chill eventually change the listener's *expectations*? Why doesn't the listener get habituated to the event in the music that follows the expectation-violation of expectation sequence? Why doesn't the surprise or shock reaction extinguish?

Here comes another speculation: The chill response, laid down by evolution, is an inherent motivation of living creatures, mothers in particular, but not exclusively, to respond to separation–distress cries of their young. A mother always needs to be immediately responsive to the distress of her off-spring. Habituation of that response to distress would go counter to the evolutionary benefits of a mother protecting her babies. The survival value of the separation–distress–vocalization–chill sequence must include that it does not extinguish easily. If it did habituate and extinguish, perhaps the first or second time a baby rat strayed away from its mother and sent out a distress call would result

38 Thrills and goose bumps in music

in the mother's response. Later calls, or the calls of subsequently born pups, would however then go unheeded. My speculation: the robust quality of the chill response derives from its evolutionary basis and value.

The good news is that my goose bump response to the Sibelius symphony or the Schubert quartet will never extinguish. I will always feel that thrill.

Chapter 3

Music as narrative

In the mysteries by Arthur Conan Doyle, clues or mini-narratives are revealed in the course of the story and then Sherlock Holmes pieces these mini-narratives together into a surprising explanation, a master narrative. I hope to do just that in this chapter: to present a number of discrete stories, and then join them in a statement about music as narrative. To argue that music can contain a narrative seems to argue against the position that music, as such, is abstract and has no meaning. I have described the argument that the expressive power of music is distinctly different from the meaning of music, that music does not have a literal meaning, that it is pure emotion. However, even as "pure" emotion music communicates between at least two people or one person within themselves. As such it has meaning to each. And, as I have also argued along with Ed Tronick (2011), people are meaning makers. And if music does have meaning, music can convey a narrative. That is the argument of this chapter.

My memory of the Bizet *Symphony in C* in my analysis only had a specific personal meaning to me. That meaning had nothing to do with any intentions of Bizet or any particular characteristics of the music. Similarly, the waltz from *The Merry Widow* had a specific meaning to me that had nothing to do with the title of the operetta. However, in both instances, the Bizet *Symphony* and *The Merry Widow*, I as a listener, gave the music a personal meaning in my personal narrative. And when I hear either of these compositions, as well as many others, my personal meaning will cross my mind. I am not alone in this. Many couples refer to a particular song as "our song" because it has acquired or is linked to a special event or has a special meaning for them. My point is that the expressive power of the music and a

DOI: 10.4324/9781003220954-4

40 Music as narrative

non-intended emotional impact collapses in the listener. What a listener, as a meaning-maker, brings is an indissoluble part of the whole music experience for each listener. The music listening experience then comprises the composer, performer, listener, and more.

A word about "meaning-making" (Tronick, 2011). Meaning-making is already a capacity of infants as they garner and process information

> to increase their complexity and coherence ... They (make) nonverbal meaning—affects, movements, representation—about themselves in relation to the world ... which shapes their ongoing engagement with the world ... their meaning-making is nonsymbolic and radically different from the representational meanings made by older children and adults.
>
> (p. 107)

Our meaning-making capacity as adults is built upon, and thereby includes, our early, nonverbal, affective, and bodily sources out of which meanings are made. After some detours, I will come back to this point.

Movie music

We are all familiar with the use of music to enhance a narrative, as, for example, background music in movies. Ideally, we should not be aware of movie music. It accompanies the action in a film by underlining and expressing emotions. For example, music in a film may accompany a vulnerable-looking person walking through a dark street. The music then can evoke and enhance feelings of alarm and terror that are intrinsic to the narrative of the film. The music Bernard Herrmann composed for Hitchcock's *Psycho*, especially for the shower scene, as presented in the previous chapter is, I believe, unforgettable. That scene would not have been so terrifying without the screeching violins. The music underlined, enhanced, and depicts the horror of that knife-slashing attack. Clearly, the music makes us feel the terror of the attack in a way that simply watching the scene in silence might not have. Without the music we might have tried to protect ourselves from experiencing the terror of the attack, but the music made us face it. In fact, the music even forced us, in the audience, to become more than just onlookers. It struck at our very core. It put us into the shower along with Janet Leigh.

Music in films is usually composed after the film has been shot. It can thus be thought of as secondary to the plot, but it is nevertheless an essential ingredient. It resonates with and intensifies the feelings, the total experience, of the viewers. The music in the movie engages its audience in a personal, even intimate, way. Even in the early days of silent movies, a pianist would accompany the film. It assured a direct personal emotional engagement by the audience.

Words and music in opera

In opera, as in movies, the music shares the stage with the narrative. The libretto of the opera, the narrative, is revealed through words, lyrics, staging, and actions, more or less. But the role of the music is more than just an accompaniment to the narrative. It is intrinsic to the words in that the music expresses and at times anticipates the emotions of the characters, as well as "inducing" and evoking feelings in the audience. The role of the human voice increases the dramatic and emotional impact of the lyrics. To argue that sung music enhances the emotions of a narrative and thereby contribute to a narrative is self-evident. Yet the music has more than an ancillary or supportive role.

The experience of listening to sung dialogue, compared to spoken dialogue, is quite different. When we listen to sung dialogue we feel it as a direct emotional experience. When we listen to spoken dialogue, we may have an emotional experience as well, but it is via a cognitive process and through our imagination. It may not seem to be quite as direct or immediate as music's path to our emotions. Or is it? Even spoken words are not affectless. The prosody in the dialogue is an intrinsic part of its communicative value. By prosody I mean the rhythmic and intonational aspect of language. Here is the link to the inevitable inclusion of music when people speak to each other. The prosody is the music that gives an emotional voice to the speaker. The speaker's emotions and intent in speaking become inseparable. The expressive and emotional power of the music are one, and the words are joined with the music and evoke an affective resonance in the listener.

Several composers have argued for parity between words and music. One such composer was Richard Wagner (1983) who wrote the libretti, which he called poetry, for all his operas, which he called music dramas. Wagner wrote extensively to support his argument that his poetry was as great as his music. However, many opera lovers, including me, consider his music to be groundbreaking and magnificent, far superior to his poetry (see Chapter 5). Yet Wagner linked his music and libretti concretely through his use of *leitmotifs*. These are short melodies that represent a character or an entity. The narrative is given complexity since a character may be singing about one thing but thinking about someone else, as expressed by the leitmotif played as part of the orchestral accompaniment.

For example, in *Das Rhinegold*, the first opera of the Ring of the Nibelungen cycle, there are motifs that depict entities such as The Rhine River, The Rhinegold, as well as Valhalla, the home for the Gods that Wotan has paid the giants to build for him. He used the stolen gold from the river Rhine, the Rhinegold, for payment since the giants initially demanded Wotan's wife's sister as the price for building Valhalla. Wotan bargained and got the giants to accept the gold instead. That is one of the stories that runs through the four operas of the Ring cycle. In Das Rhinegold, the first opera Alberich steals the gold that is being guarded by the three Rhinemaidens.

YouTube Video
Der Ring Des Nibelungen: Das Rheingold [Boulez]—English subs

Composer Richard Strauss wrote an opera, *Capriccio*, about a composer and a poet. Both woo the same young woman. She has to decide which suitor she prefers, and the opera ends just before she announces her decision. To announce her decision would require Strauss to indicate a preference of music over words, or the reverse. So, he ends the opera before she reveals her decision, whom she loves more, and by extension, which is more important, words or music. Strauss indicates that to express a preference for one over the other is arbitrary. Each has a distinct, unique role when both are equally involved. Once music and words are united, the narrative is told by both with the music spelling out the emotional impact of the narrative. Or, put differently, the words add language and specific meaning to the emotions conveyed by the music, thus eventuating in a narrative.

YouTube Video
Renee Fleming in *Capricio*

These considerations lead us to another but related question. Can music alone, without words, tell a story on its own? This is the question to which I now turn.

Program music and absolute music

Music in movies, operas, and songs is referred to as program music and can be contrasted with absolute music (Haas, 1984). This distinction is relevant for our discussion. Whereas program music is linked to words and thus parallels a narrative in words, absolute music has no associated words and the music itself must thus carry a narrative, if indeed it can.

We respond to program music because its underlying story or plot is as important as the music itself. Examples of program music include the afore-mentioned Franz Lehar operetta *The Merry Widow* and Ludwig van Beethoven's *Sixth Symphony, The Pastoral*. Musical passages in the Beethoven symphony depict a shepherd calling to a shepherdess and other passages depict a thunderstorm. There are no words, either spoken or sung in this symphony, but with its title the symphony conveys a love for the outdoors and for a simple country life.

YouTube Video
Beethoven Symphony # 6 The Pastoral

Other examples of program music include the tone poems of Richard Strauss to which he gave titles that referred to books and literary topics. Except for the titles, no words tell the story of *Don Quixote* or *Don Juan*. But as we will see in Chapter 7, Richard Strauss tells complex stories just through his music in his tone poems. Other illustrations might be Antonio Vivaldi's *The Four Season* and Tchaikovsky's *1812 Overture*. In each of these works we can discern a narrative in the music as implied by the title and other clues provided by the composer. In these examples the clues are both in a word language as well as in the use of culturally well-known referents. For example, as I have already

44 Music as narrative

described, Tchaikovsky used the French Anthem *La Marseillaise* to depict the French defeat by the Russians in the War of 1812.

YouTube Video
Tchaikovsky 1812 Overture

La Marseillaise occupies quite a different meaning in the narrative of the film, *Casablanca.* When the German soldiers sing their anthem, *Vaterland*, Humphrey Bogart (Rick) signals to the band in his bar to play *La Marseillaise* to drown out the German's song. It is a highpoint of the film because hitherto Rick had claimed to be apolitical. When questioned about his politics he said he was a "drunkard." In signaling the band to play the French anthem he made a commitment to the Free French cause. The battle of the bands, as this scene is usually called (McKee, 1997), tells a complex story just through the music.

YouTube Video
La Marseillaise, Battle of the Bands *Casablanca*

All these musical illustrations fall within the category of Program Music. They also illustrate the range of personal, cultural, divergent, and universal meanings that music can evoke, or acquire, depending on its context. In contrast we enjoy Absolute Music in and of itself. It is here that the music itself must provide a narrative, if it can. Many of Mozart and Haydn's symphonies, as well as the afore-mentioned Bizet symphony, are good examples of this genre.

Along came Beethoven

Alas, the dividing line between program and absolute music is not so sharp. In his *Sixth Symphony*, Beethoven shook the distinction between program and absolute music. In his *Ninth Symphony* he shattered the tradition of symphonic absolute music laid down by Haydn and Mozart by including, in its *Fourth Movement*, a chorus and soloists to proclaim "Alle Maenschen werden Brueder" (All mankind will become brothers). After its first performance in 1824, words sung by soloists and a chorus were used more liberally in symphonic music as, for example, in several of the symphonies of Gustav Mahler. The boundary between program and absolute music was and continues to be further blurred.

The first three movements of Beethoven's *Ninth Symphony* seem to be purely absolute, symphonic music. However, not quite. The *First Movement* begins with an "open fifth." An open fifth refers to the orchestra playing the first and fifth notes of the musical scale but not including the crucial third note. The third note identifies the composition's key signature, either in a major or minor key. Music written in a major key, as I have been emphasizing, tends to be rousing, stern, and/or joyful. Music written in a minor key tends to be sad and evoke feelings of yearning, melancholy, and longing. Not identifying the key leaves the listener wondering and wandering, somewhat bewildered, perhaps even looking for an emotional home. Thereby the *First Movement*, the opening of the *Ninth Symphony*, begins by raising questions, uncertainty, and ambiguity in the listener's mind: "Where are we? What is happening? Where are we going?" A narrative has begun just by the orchestra articulating these questions.

Leonard Bernstein (1982) described this opening as "formless chaos" (p. 292). It leaves the listeners in a state of uncertainty, but, as Bernstein argues, it also gives the conductor an enormous range of possibilities as to how to shape this work. More than the narrator of a story, the conductor has considerable interpretive latitude, constrained only broadly by the composer and the markings on the score. That is, conductors can shape the work along quite different musical narratives. Bernstein holds that different performances can follow the opening bars of the Beethoven *Ninth Symphony* depending on how the conductor tells the story. To illustrate, Bernstein describes two very different performances of the *Ninth Symphony* that he conducted within four days of each other. He conducted the first one in Vienna and second one in Boston. He considered the Vienna performance to be more romantic, from the opening chaos culminating in the "development of man in full reason and spirit, complete with ... dynamic exaggerations and/or vacillating tempi, poetical meanderings, and personal subjective indulgences" (p. 292). In contrast, he described his Boston performance as

> highly literal, faithful rhythmically and a dynamically accurate reading of the score, free of orchestral changes or additions, without gratuitous abuses or retardations ... faithful even to

46 Music as narrative

> (Beethoven's) highly controversial ... metronomic markings, and with no dynamic adjustments in the cause of orchestral balance.
>
> (p. 292)

Bernstein ascribed the different performances to his taking advantage of the different acoustics of the concert halls in Vienna and Boston, the different makes of the instruments used by the musicians, German instrument makers in one case compared to American makers of the Boston's instruments, as well as the differing musical traditions of the two orchestras. Bernstein indirectly points to the essential co-creation of artistic productions: by the artist, the métier used by the artist, and the environment (including audience) in which the art is displayed. Such co-creating opens the door to constructing different narratives out of the same composition.

To return to Beethoven's *Ninth Symphony*, after the chaotic, bewildering opening movement that can leave the listener wandering and wondering throughout the next movements, Beethoven searches for answers to his posed questions: Where are we? Where are we going? In the subsequent movements he offers assertive, percussive, romantic, and longing themes as tentative responses. Then, in the last movement Beethoven briefly reprises the themes from the three preceding movements and has the orchestra resoundingly reject each of them. Ascribing a meaning, "rejection" to that orchestral music already ascribes a narrative to what is ostensibly absolute music. The orchestra's rejection of the three themes anticipates the tenor who then does so in words. Following the same melodic line with which the orchestra has just rejected the themes of the first three movements, Beethoven has the tenor offer a literal response to the opening question: He sings: "No not these tones. Let us find others."

Standing alone, the first three movements are absolute music. But, even without the words of the fourth movement, the first three movements do have a narrative. That is, a narrative in the form of a conversation that begins in the first movement and is carried solely by the orchestra in the music. Without using words, the music of the first three movements presents a narrative to depict searching man. The last movement offers a solution, a brotherhood of mankind, a glorious union among all people.

My point is that program and absolute music overlap and a sharp division cannot be drawn any longer between them. But, more to the point, once you have engaged the emotions of the listener, you have created an implicit, personal, and perhaps even universal narrative. In his *Ninth Symphony*, Beethoven created a narrative through "dialogue" among the movements of the symphony and between the soloist and the orchestra. It is a conversation between the earlier themes and the later ones, resounding rejection of these, first by the orchestra and then, in words, by the tenor, followed by the chorus.

Bernstein conducted Beethoven's *Ninth Symphony* with an orchestra composed of musicians from East and West Germany when the Berlin wall was taken down. For that occasion, he also changed one of the words of the chorus. Instead of singing "freude" he had them sing "freiheit."

YouTube Video
Beethoven Symphony # 9.
Bernstein Cond.

Conversation, dialogue, and the concerto

In his *Ninth Symphony*, Beethoven initially composed a dialogue just in the music, before using words. He composed similar musical dialogues in other works as well.

Dialogues and even conflict between instruments or groups of instruments were found in music way before Beethoven. The concerto has been described as a composition for two opposing and unequal forces (Siegmeister, 1945). Once you pit a single instrument, or a small group of instruments against a larger group, as Bach did in his Brandenburg Concertos, you have a "conflict" and hence a story, a narrative.

YouTube Video
Bach Brandenburg Concerto # 3

The challenge the composer sets up is to compose a musical dialogue in which the solo instrument or small group of instruments, strive for

48   Music as narrative

an equal voice in musical weight to the orchestral larger and hence musically more powerful group. And the net effect has to be artistically and musically sound, not just a beautiful orchestral accompaniment for a small group of instruments or a solo violin or piano.

In Chapter 2, I already referred to Beethoven's *Piano Concerto in G # 4 in that it* offers another illustration of a dialogue without the use of words, just through music. Another illustration is offered by Leonard Bernstein (1976) in his analysis of Beethoven's *Sonata op. 31 #3*. In this sonata for solo piano Bernstein imagines a conversation just in the piano part. He "hears" one part of the melody as a plea, "Please, I implore you, I will do anything ..." as though from one lover pleading to a partner not to be left. From the other lover Bernstein imagines a hesitant response in the melody, "Yes, but only under certain conditions." The specific narrative imagined by Bernstein is unlikely to be Beethoven's intent. But Bernstein did construct or impose a personal narrative on the music and many listeners hear the opening of the second movement of the piano concerto as a conversation between the string instruments and the piano. Hearing this music as a dialogue or conversation also gives it a personal meaning. The expressive power and the meaning of the music become indistinguishable for the listener.

Bernstein emphasizes that the conductor or pianist playing the music can infuse a personal narrative into what may appear to be absolute music. A listener, as I did with the Bizet and Lehar compositions, can do this as well. Like the conductor, the listener can feel the music in any way that has personal meaning. However, the conductor is under some constraint in interpreting the music since some knowledge of the composer's intentions is crucial. But there is even considerable leeway here. How the composer's intentions are understood will resonate differently with different conductors. And, of course, there is also considerable leeway based on how the conductor feels the music or feels into the narrative in the score. Thus, no two performances of the same piece by the same conductor or the same piece by different conductors will ever be alike.

Looked at from the vantage point of the conductor, every piece of music tells a musical narrative that may or may not be translated into words. If we argue that the conductor inserts a narrative into the music, then perhaps we can agree that music does not exist without a performer or listener. Even if we look at the written score of a composition, it does not come alive without our reading or performing it. And as soon as we introduce a person, we have introduced a meaning-making entity, as well as an affective/emotional resonator. Then we are back in the arena of subjectivity, affect, and yes, we have created a narrative. With the emphasis on meaning and narrative we have inserted the role of language into this discussion.

Oliver Sachs has something to say or rather to sing

Samuel S. had a stroke in his late 60s and thereafter developed severe expressive aphasia (Sachs, 2008). Speech therapy to restore his ability to use language was attempted but did not restore his ability to communicate verbally. The stroke had resulted in severe damage to the parts of the brain responsible for language. In spite of extensive speech therapy, he was totally unable to speak and was unable to "retrieve a single word" (p. 232). Apparently by chance, the music therapist of the hospital in which Oliver Sachs worked and Samuel S. resided heard him singing *Ol' Man River* outside her office. He sang "very tunefully and with great feeling, but only getting two or three words of the song" (p. 232).

Samuel S. had previously been deemed hopeless by the speech therapist but this serendipitous observation by the music therapist gave her hope. She began to work with him on a three-times-a-week basis for half hour session. These sessions consisted of the therapist singing with him or accompanying him on her accordion. Samuel S. soon recovered all the words to *Ol' Man River* and many other songs he had learned growing up. What, however, was most astonishing was his recovery of speech during this time. He could now answer simple question, which he had been unable to do previously. For example, when he was asked about his weekend at home he could respond, "saw the kids" (p. 233). Working on his recovery of songs had simultaneously freed his ability to recover words.

Sachs distinguishes between aphasia, loss of speech and language, and amuse, an inability to recognize or reproduce music. Some brain damage may result in aphasia, as in the case of Samuel S. but not in amuse. When someone asked another of Sachs's patients, Mrs. L, what does she hear when music is played, she answered, "if you were in my kitchen and threw all the pots and pans on the floor, that's what I hear" (p. 112). She suffered from amuse but not aphasia. Sachs hereby illustrated the separation of the brain areas for speech and music.

Sachs also offers an important distinction between therapy for motor disorders such as Parkinsonism and speech disorders such as aphasia. In the former where music and rhythm are also used to regain lost motor functions, CDs and tapes of music work well to restore these functions. Not so with aphasia. There the relationship between the therapist and the patient plays a crucial part. Sachs cites the Russian neurologist Luria for emphasizing "the origin of speech was social no less neurological—it required the interaction of mother and child" (p. 238). With that statement the crucial role of affective human communication is recognized as central to the re-acquisition of speech. By invoking early mother–infant communication, the door is opened to the inherent role of prosody in human communication that links music to speech acquisition.

According to Sachs a personal interaction is necessary for speech acquisition. He argues that Samuel S. listening to CDs or tapes of *Ol' Man River* could not have begun his road back to speech. It required the participation of a living person, the music therapist. Sachs, in referencing Luria, recognizes the crucial role of mother–infant communication in the acquisition of speech, and to that we can now add, the acquisition of speech through music.

Mothers speak motherese to their babies

Mothers speak to their infants in a special sing-song language called "motherese." The communication to which Luria referred already contains a special vocal twist that adults habitually add when speaking to infants. And as I will soon discuss, the infant responds musically as well. It makes perfect sense that the re-acquisition of words requires a human interaction to replicate the initial learning of language that includes the musicality of the human voice. But there is more. Joe Lichtenberg, Jim Fosshage, and I (Lichtenberg, Lachmann and Fosshage, 2016) described neonates and infants as beginning life "bathed in the sounds of human speech and washed in the sounds of music" (p. 32). We cited Panksepp (1998) who stated, "musical affective prosody engages the communicative efforts of infants more than any imaginative-propositional thought" (pp. 47–48).

> Parents the world over follow the same essential pattern of talking to infants, a pattern as tuned to an infant's receptive capacity as any design could make it. Parent's prattle, their "motherese," is characterized by syntactic simplicity, segmentation, a slow tempo, a limited repertoire of highly repetitive expressive melodic patterns enhanced by pitch variations using endings with an overall rise.
>
> (Lichtenberg, Lachmann, and Fosshage, 2016, p. 32)

Relevant for the present discussion is that motherese is rich in musicality and that it piggybacks words onto the music. In this way the melody of the words can form a "… musical prosodic bridge to the infant's right cerebral hemisphere language development" (Woodhead, 2010, p. 52). Motherese seems to be a more sophisticated version of the Neanderthal's "hmmmmmmm," ideally suited for bonding and connecting affectively with the baby.

Babies sing "Mm, Mm" to their mothers

Like Ralph Greenson (1947, Lachmann, 2014a), Leonard Bernstein (1976) also came up with a similar speculation some years later about the "mmmmm," but from an entirely different source. He discovered a series of notes that resembled the "mm" sound in music from different countries around the globe. Bernstein also related this sound to the sound a baby can make and not lose any milk. And both he and Greenson agreed that the word "mother" in many languages begins with this "mm" sound. Bernstein also found another series of notes that resembled an "ech" sound, which he suggested was "spitting out the bad milk." Both Bernstein and Greenson assume an interaction between a mother and baby with the baby expressing either pleasure or disgust. And both Greenson and Bernstein have thus proposed similar ideas about the origins of music in the "mm, mm" sound and the mother–infant relationship, topics to which we now turn.

On the origins of music

The speculations of Greenson and Bernstein about the "mm" sound can be linked to the origins of music as discussed by Steven Mithens (2006) from an evolutionary perspective and by Jaak Panksepp (1998) who also addressed our evolution-based response to music. A third contributor to this topic is, who else, but Leonard Bernstein (1976). In his Norton Lectures he refers to the work of linguist, philosopher, and cognitive scientist Noam Chomsky on innate grammar. Bernstein applies Chomsky's proposal of an innate structure that is found in poetry and applies it to the structure of music. It is this innate structure that enables us to resonate with music.

Steven Mithens, a Professor of early history, writing from an evolutionary standpoint, gathered from descriptions of the skeletal size and bodily capacities of Neanderthals, as well as from the structures in their throat and chest, that there is "… compelling evidence for a capacity to form and express an advanced 'Hmmmmmm' sound" (p. 228). He uses that "hmmmmmm" designation because he considers the use of either the words "music" or "language" at that point in time to be misleading. Rather, he holds that music and language shared a common prehistoric origin. He argues that music, varying that "hmmmmmm" sound tonally, once provided the underlying glue for human communication as far back as Neanderthal times. Because the Neanderthals lived in relatively small and highly stable communities, communication and cooperation became possible and began to flourish. Their ability to vary their "hmmmmm" did not confine communication to pointing. They could add various kinds of grunts, which gave them opportunities for joint ventures. They could make both sounds, mimic, and point, as for example, "hunt animal with me … or share food with … followed by a pointing gesture toward an individual or a mimesis of the individual" (p. 172). Through their more evolved capacity to make the "hmmmmmm" sounds, Mithens proposed that Neanderthals were able to form more lasting bonds with each other than had been possible for other tribes. By lasting bonds he implies emotional connections thereby giving tonal vocalizations a prime role in forming bonds. As to the question, which came first, language or music, the straight grunts or the tonally varied "hmmmmmm," Mithens holds they had a common origin. Mithens thus also provides evidence for the bonding

Music as narrative 53

and communicative power of music. And Mithens, like Bernstein, argues that music does not "mean" anything. It is pure emotion, the language of emotions. In that case there cannot be a narrative in music, per se, but we shall see.

Music, affect, and narrative

In the beginning there was "Hmmmmmm." It was the beginning of communication, a sound that could be varied and would evolve into words and music. The sound was made by the just-evolving human voice and enabled the Neanderthals to communicate, cooperate, bond, and alert each other to danger. From this common origin in which communication entailed no distinction between word sounds and tonal variation, we evolved to have brains in which language and music came to occupy different areas. Imagine how certain grunts could evolve to become words to impart information and how varying these grunts could convey an affective dimension to the grunts and become "music." In this way, the ability of the Neanderthals to bond and make connections within their tribe furthered the eventual formation of more cohesive groups. This evolution could lead to rituals and other group events that enabled the tribe to remember and celebrate its "narrative" history.

From current neurological studies we know that the brain evolved to locating language and music in different areas. Presumably, this specialization increased survival value. But, although they have come to occupy different areas in the brain, language and music are re-united in early mother–infant communication through motherese, the way mothers speak with a special intonation to their babies. From birth, we and our brains integrate language and music. The integration furthers our meaning-making propensity and enables us to tell narratives of our life with music, which means we can sing, that is, talk with affect.

Why is "motherese" so universally and unselfconsciously adopted by mothers as they speak to their babies? Intuitively, the lilt, cadence, timing, and the embedded musicality of motherese conveys positive affect, safety, and, most importantly makes a direct affective connection with the infant. In this sense motherese may be a descendent from the Neanderthals "Hmmmmmm" that enhanced their communication and bonding. But attachments are co-created (Beebe and Lachmann,

2015) and for their part, the infants contribute gurgles, laughter, and, at times, even "mm" sounds of their own. The baby signals through its own language/music, its own affective state, and communicates the satisfying experience of holding on to mother's milk. Ironically, then too, the baby's "mm" may harken back to Neanderthal communication that led to bonding in prehistoric times.

Whether through gurgles or laughter the baby's sounds also have a prosody that engages affectively with the mother. The separate brain areas for language and music of mother and infant are thus both engaged, simultaneously, through the mother's and infant's communication. This bi-directional emotional engagement promotes the integration of language and music and makes the interaction a human, "alive" event. As Oliver Sachs has shown, music alone or words alone cannot restore lost language. The restoration of linguistic ability must replicate the original acquisition of speech that occurred through the mother–infant relationship, through their "collaborative" dialogue (Lyons-Ruth, 1999).

Panksepp's work on the separation–longing–distress–reunion sequence, as discussed in Chapter 2, demonstrates that sounds and music do acquire meaning. They become a narrative laid down by evolution. When that sequence is repeated, either deliberately or inadvertently in music, the music makes a beeline to our emotions. It directly accesses our affective life. We respond emotionally, neurologically, anatomically, and physiologically. We may even get goose bumps when we hear certain musical compositions, or rather certain specific occurrences in musical compositions that resemble the shock and surprise, the violation of expectation that mothers experiences when they hear a distress call from their infants. The sequence engages us in an effective communication that includes our whole body and to which we attribute a meaning.

Have you noticed, as I did after reviewing the various mini narratives, that many of the musical illustrations I have included, so far, turn out to be separations and reunions. My memories of the waltz from the *Merry Widow* and the Bizet Symphony were prompted by separation and longings and served as symbols of reunion. The opening of the Beethoven *Ninth Symphony* depicting "searching man" leads to the brotherhood of all men, and the dialogue that Bernstein injected into the Beethoven Piano Sonata was about longing and loss.

Music is well suited to capture our feelings of longing and loss through minor keys and reunion through major keys. In addition, a surprising shift in the music, a new voice coming in can signal that distress. Our emotions are activated as are our physiological states and sensory impressions. Goose bumps are clear evidence that such activation has occurred, and we are back, again, in our evolutionary heritage.

When we ascribe meaning to an experience we do so with our integrated meaning-making brains. We thereby create a narrative. In the separation–distress–reunion sequence we are creating a narrative that contributes to security in attachment to others, just as the "hmmmmmm" contributed to the Neanderthal's affiliation within their group. In these instances, we achieve an increased sense of competence and mastery over our world.

I have spelled out a connection among music, affect, and meaning. Meaning-making provides the direct link to narrative construction. Through engaging affect, music acquires meaning, and thereby creates a narrative. Then the direct path of music to our emotions can prompt us to construct a personal narrative or a shared narrative. However, is that narrative really an intrinsic part of the music or is it imposed on the music by the listener? We have revisited the question: is there absolute music or is it a question of degrees of programmatic music?

The narrative embedded in the first three movement of Beethoven's *Ninth Symphony* is clearly Beethoven's doing, but what about the dialogue Bernstein "heard" in the Beethoven Piano Sonata? That was a personal dialogue "imposed" on the music. Or, as I suggested earlier, did the affect elicited by the music lend itself to being experienced, in Bernstein's words, as a "separation–longing" experience. The conversation Bernstein read into the sonata falls short of a goose bump or chill moment but does lend itself to capturing feelings of yearning and longing.

In the case of the Bizet *Symphony* and *La Marseilles,* a personal and a shared narrative, what the music has come to mean may not have been the composer's intention. But, once composed, when the music connects with the listener's emotions, the composer is no longer in control of the music. It has now become the property of each listener, some of who will ascribe different narratives to the same music. Even if the composer has ascribed a program to the composition and the music evokes strong feelings in the listener, it acquires a personal

56 Music as narrative

meaning for the listener. That's what I did with the waltz from *The Merry Widow*. This affective impact of a composition opens the door to that composition acquiring a narrative by some listeners, and perhaps a similar or a different narrative from other.

From the vantage point that music in and of itself conveys an affectively rooted meaning and therefore, a narrative, an indissoluble unit is formed. This unit includes the conductor, performer, composer, composition, listener, and even the make of the instruments and acoustics of the hall in which it is performed. The composer has unleashed an affective experience and is responsible for his intent and not responsible for its impact on the listener's experience. Beethoven is responsible for the open fifth he composed at the beginning of his *Ninth Symphony*. The emotionally moved listener is a meaning-maker who contributes the narrative to the music. In some compositions that narrative may be as vague as coming out of dark, dreary countryside and into sunlight, or a reunion after a scary separation. It can be as simple as that, or more complex when, for example, the music evokes a whole scenario of combating and triumphing over aggression—whether this refers to Napoleon's army in Russia or to the Nazis in Casablanca.

Once affect is engaged, music inevitably acquires a meaning, which may be quite subjective, unlike the meanings one finds for words in a dictionary. This subjective meaning clearly applies to the program music such as the waltz from *The Merry Widow* and *La Marseillaise*. But meaning and narrative also apply to the dialogues or "conflict" in a concerto. Once we have imposed a term like dialogue on the music, we have made, constructed, or discerned a narrative in the music.

Where are we? Even though words or language and music occupy different areas in the brain, from birth we have integrated them beginning with the affective connection between mothers and infants. From the vantage point of subsequent development, listening to music moves us affectively and that experience has meaning and constitutes a narrative. Language and meaning are an intricate part of our musical experience. It works the other way round as well. When we speak unless we include music in our speech, we will sound "boring."

We begin life with words and music, as the package of communication, and that has been true since prehistoric times. It is the music that is attached to our words that engages us and our partners in communication. From prehistoric times on, music, in some form, has been part of our speech. Words without music are disembodied. As a package, words and music give meaning to our communications and that is the essence of a narrative and that enables us to form emotional bonds with each other.

Chapter 4

Richard Wagner
Childhood trauma and creativity

Richard Wagner lost two fathers early in his life. His biological father was pretty clear, much to Richard's regret. He was Ludwig Geyer, a painter, actor, and poet who lived in the Wagner house. And, much to Richard's later dismay, he may have been a Jew. The other father, Carl Friedrich Wagner, was married to Johanna, Richard's mother, and he died before Richard reached the age of one. Richard's mother then married Ludwig Geyer.

Carl Friedrich Wagner had been a police official and had an active interest in literature, poetry, and theater. His interest in the theater evidently specialized in actresses and Johanna told her son that he flirted with all of them and "… often came home later than expected while he paid rapturous visits to a certain actress of the day" (Wagner, 1983, p. 3). He would offer the excuse that he was detained on business and showed Johanna his ink-stained fingers as evidence. But, Johanna said jokingly, as Richard recalled, that his fingers were always clean.

Johanna was 35 when Richard was born. She suffered from a head ailment that required her to wear a cap. She must have been pretty when young as evidenced by her portrait and apparently she had remained attractive to men. In retrospect Richard said of his mother, "I hardly ever remember being caressed by her, outpouring of affection did not occur in our family. (Rather) … a certain impetuous, even loud and boisterous manner characterized our family" (Wagner, 1983, p. 11). Richard recalled being taken to bed one night by his mother and a visitor. She spoke with "strange zeal … of the great and beautiful in art but she did not include drama among these, only poetry, music, and painting" (p. 11). In fact, reported Richard, "she came close to threatening me with her curse if ever I too were to think of going

DOI: 10.4324/9781003220954-5

Childhood trauma and creativity 59

into the theater" (p. 12). Having had a husband who spent time with actresses probably made her wary about losing her son to actresses also.

Also living in the Wagner household was Ludwig Geyer. As Carl Friedrich often spent time in the arms of actresses, Johanna apparently found solace in the arms of young Geyer. After Richard's birth, when Johanna had recovered from her confinement, she left her husband and made a perilous journey of over 150 miles with 6 children and 2 babies—one being Richard—to see Geyer. Presumably, Carl Friedrich had wanted nothing to do with young Richard. Eventually, Johanna and Carl Friedrich worked something out and Johanna returned to Carl Friedrich. Carl Friedrich then acknowledged Richard as his own son. Three months later, before Richard had his first birthday, Carl Friedrich died of typhus. Nine months later, Geyer married Johanna and 6 months after the wedding a girl, Cecilie, was born. Assuming that Geyer was Richard's biological father, she would have been Richard's only full sister. She became his favorite playmate and companion.

When he was three months old, Richard was baptized. That fact could still leave the question of his paternity ambiguous. So, in his autobiography Wagner wrote that he was christened two days after he was born as though Carl Friedrich Wagner never had any doubt about Richard being his son.

After Carl Friedrich's death, when Geyer married Johanna he took care of her and all her children. Cecilie was then on the way and there was no doubt about Geyer being her father. Geyer became a devoted husband and father and was most caring of all the Wagner children. He died when Richard was nine years old.

When Richard went to school, he was called Richard Geyer. Even though Ludwig Geyer by all accounts was a devoted caretaker of all the Wagner children, after Geyer's death, when he was 14 years old, Richard rejected the Geyer name. He falsified information about his baptism and referred to himself as Richard Wagner. As an adult, Wagner confided to Nietzsche that he did believe that he was Geyer's son. The reason for the name change? Again, speculation among Wagner scholars: Geyer was a name held by Jews—not all Geyers were Jews— but enough were to prompt Richard to reject this connection in order to retain his "racial purity." This was only one of many falsifications in Wagner's autobiography. In fact, some of his biographers agree it is pure fiction. Irvine (1911) wrote a treatise on this autobiography titled, "Wagner's Bad Luck" in which he identified 800 errors in this autobiography. The autobiography is really more revealing in its psychological truths and the myths Wagner sought to perpetuate about himself, than about biographical and historical accuracy.

Another falsification in the autobiography is Wagner's claim that unlike his brothers and sisters he was not given a musical education. He claimed that this was the result of his having been considered lacking musical talent. He claimed that he then taught himself to play the piano and figured out how to play some of the music from the then-popular Carl Maria von Weber opera, *Der Freischütz*.

YouTube Video
Von Weber Overture, Der Freischütz

As Ludwig Geyer lay on his deathbed, Johanna asked 9-year-old Richard to play the piano for his father. He played two folk songs and an aria from *Der Freischütz*. Astonished, his dying father remarked, "Is it possible he has a musical talent?" (Wagner, 1983, p. 9).

There is one further incident that contributes to the chaotic, traumatic ambiguities in Richard's early life. Wagner reports in his autobiography, and this entry has not been disputed, that shortly after his birth, he was found to suffer from a common ailment of infancy. He was so sick that his mother, as she later told him, almost wished him "dead owing to his seemingly hopeless condition. I seemed to have surprised my parents by thriving" (p. 5). Wagner reported that his parents (Johanna and Carl Friedrich) were astonished by his subsequent good health. Later, in his adult life, he frequently suffered from a skin condition, erysipelas, that made his existence miserable. This is an inflammatory disease of the upper layers of the skin. Symptoms may include fever and chills and swollen "glands" or lymph nodes. The skin can be painful, red, and tender with blister and scab. Such chronic personal discomfort added to the impact of the early chaotic circumstances of his home. In his opera *Siegfried*, the title character acquires a protective, almost impenetrable skin covering. It makes him almost invulnerable. In acquiring his impenetrable skin covering, a leaf falls on Siegfried's shoulder leaving him with one vulnerable spot.

Childhood trauma and creativity 61

In several ways Richard Wagner, having been a sickly child, may well have been attracted to the glorification of powerful men like Siegfried, Tannhauser, and Wotan who hovers over the four-opera cycle, *The Ring of the Niebelungen*. Yet all his heroes had some vulnerability. The music he wrote was well matched to their exalted power and strength.

Both of Richard Wagner's parents apparently had lovers quite openly although Johanna seemed to have tolerated Carl Friedrich's affairs better than Carl Friedrich did Johanna's. Perhaps through his lies, deceptions, and falsifications Richard Wagner attempted to normalize or justify the chaotic world in which he grew up. But to do so he had to invent his history and betray the devoted Geyer. Furthermore, in his life and art he elevated infidelity and betrayal. Tristan and Isolde betray Isolde's intended King Mark. There are betrayals and infidelities galore in the Ring cycle, and in *Tannhauser* the epitome of passion is achieved with the Goddess Venus, not with Elizabeth. Redemption either came through the sacrifice of women or had to wait until after death.

Although Geyer seemed to have been a decent person, the other adults in Richard's life were motivated by self-interest and opportunism. Geyer's reputation was no match for the more charismatic Carl Friedrich, at least as he was funneled through Johanna's description of him to Richard. Contacts among the adults in the Wagner–Geyer household were sustained more through sexual liaisons than affectionate relations. Richard did not think of his mother as ever having caressed and soothed him sensually. From the description of his home, the sound level seemed to have been boisterous or rather fortissimo. On one hand, all these characteristics would speak to the Wagner home being maintained at a high level of arousal with little opportunity to tone-down. On the other hand, it all led to composing operas that required an extra-large orchestra and singers with voices powerful enough to rise above that orchestra.

There are no indications that the Wagner's home was in any way violent or one in which the children suffered from neglect or deprivation with respect to food, clothing, or shelter. But inconsistencies, ambiguities, and mixed messages abounded, beginning with the question specific only to Richard: "Who is my father?" It is important to note that Richard was the only one whose paternity was in doubt. The children born before him were all Wagners and Cecilie was a Geyer.

62 Childhood trauma and creativity

But, most important, Richard's early "near, shortly-after-birth, death" experience is of special significance. Whatever the actuality, the family story that his mother almost wished he would die, and how overjoyed the parents were upon his survival, remained a myth that was often repeated by Richard Wagner and his mother.

Surviving an early brush with death is the kind of experience that also appears in the life of some other creative artists, for example, Chagall, Stravinsky, and Picasso (see Lachmann, 2008). Whatever imprint the actual experience made, we cannot know, but the myth that the family wove around this event lived on for the child. And judging by the work and life of Wagner and these other artists, the family myth reinforced a belief, a pervasive organizing principle:

> I am a violator of expectations. My family expected me to die but I survived and they were overjoyed at my survival. I am special. In fact I am an exception to the rules and laws of societal conventions. I expect the world to be as overjoyed at my presence as my family was at my remaining alive.

The story of Wagner's alleged self-taught musical ability and his early survival of a near-death experience can be seen as myths–memories–fantasies. From them another model scene can be constructed that provides a leitmotif for Wagner's life. "I am destined to be a genius. My family recognized this and I believe it. I am the family's *wunderkind*." Perhaps more accurately, as it turned out, he became a wunder-enfant terrible.

As an artist, like Stravinsky and Chagall, Richard Wagner plays with, teases, and violates the expectations of his audience (Lachmann, 2008). For Wagner, the themes of shocking and mocking conventionality, defying authority, and betraying loyalties were prominent in many of his operas. They are central to the four operas comprising *The Ring of the Niebelungen, Tristan und Isolde, Tannhauser,* and *Die Meistersinger*. The latter is the only one of his operas with roots in German History and is considered to be Wagner's most autobiographical work.

The belief in his specialness, that he was not bound by the rules and behavior that applied to ordinary people, characterized Richard Wagner throughout his life. An incident already at age 10 depicts his

Childhood trauma and creativity   63

youthful cunning and previewed as well as was replicated repeatedly in the years that follow.

From an early age on, Richard Wagner demonstrated a pomposity that invited mockery and derision. But as we shall see, he later attributed this quality to the villains, in his work, often Jews. His heroes were of pure North European stock and remain unsullied by motives of greed and deception.

Ten-year-old Richard wanted to recreate Grillparzer's classic drama *Sappho* in a "spectacular performance" (Newman, 1946, p. 12) in a puppet theater that Geyer had built for him. Richard's sisters discovered the manuscript of the play he had written and humiliated him for his pretensions and pomposity. His sisters would enrage him by tauntingly reciting his lines.

Wagner's fascination with the theater flourished during his early teen years. He was most impressed by Weber's opera *Der Freischütz*. He wrote,

> The excitement of horror and fear of ghosts constituted a singular factor in the development of my emotional life. I remember when I was alone in a room for any length of time and looked fixedly at such inanimate objects as pieces of furniture, I would suddenly burst into loud shrieks because they seemed to me to come alive. Until late in my boyhood no night passed without my awakening with a frightful scream from some dream about ghosts, which would end only when a human voice bade me be quiet. Severe scolding or even corporeal punishment would then seem to me redeeming kindnesses. None of my brothers and sisters wanted to sleep near me; they tried to bed me down as far from the others as possible, not stopping to think that by so doing my nocturnal calls to be saved from ghosts would become even louder and more enduring, until they finally accustomed themselves to this nightly calamity.
>
> (p. 13)

Wagner explained that his interest for the theater "was not so much the desire for entertainment and diversion … but rather a tingling delight in an atmosphere (that was) purely fantastic and almost appallingly attractive and lifted me (into) that fascinating demonical realm" (p. 13).

64 Childhood trauma and creativity

From these early recollections, it was but a short step to his fascination with the fantastic that later became the essence of his libretti. In effect, he subjected his audiences to an entertainment derived from his nightmares while his orchestra transformed his noisy, chaotic home into a thrilling sound scape.

From Wagner's autobiography and his biographers, we get scant clues as to why he should have suffered from such severe night terrors. I can imagine that they may have referred to his early near-death experience in the larger context of his boisterous family, unaffectionate mother, the humiliation from his siblings, as well as his unsightly and painful skin condition.

From Wagner's autobiography and the biographies, we are left with the impression that young Richard felt very much alone, shunned, and mocked by his siblings, he felt both angry and helpless. In compensation he developed character traits of grandiosity, entitlement, and pomposity that served to isolate him even further. However, his musical talent provided an entry into a world that enabled him to triumph over his detractors and provided him with the recognition and admiration he so desperately sought since childhood.

At age 13, Richard and his family moved to Dresden because his older sister had obtained a singing engagement there. Richard was sent to live in the home of school friends. Here he was surrounded by women, the sisters of his schoolmates. Family and friends with daughters came to visit the family.

> I remember pretending to be in a state of stupefied sleepiness in order to induce girls to carry me to my bed, as I had noticed to my excited surprise that their attention in similar circumstances brought me into delightfully intimate contact with the female being.
>
> (p. 16)

Richard's pretense here may point to the beginning of another theme that was to characterize the extent to which the adult Wagner betrayed his friends: plotting and subterfuge to get a woman, someone's wife, whom he wanted.

In Dresden, Richard was enrolled in a school and rebelled against the "arrogant pedantic system of instruction." Sometime later, in

Childhood trauma and creativity 65

Leipzig he applied to the better of the two schools that were available to him, but the school authorities put him back half a year. He felt indescribably disgusted and deeply wounded.

> I henceforth comported myself in such a manner as never to win the friendship of a teacher in this school. The hostile treatment I was accorded in return made me even more stubborn ... (and I developed) ... an ever increasing love of rebellion for its own sake.
>
> (p. 22)

Wagner's adolescence took the quality of a grand defiance of academic expectations. He rebelled against schoolwork even when he realized his neglect would lead to his expulsion. In secret he wrote a self-described "masterpiece." He was encouraged in this grand plan, in part, through his association with his uncle Adolph (Carl Friedrich's brother) whom he idealized as a free spirit and with whom he took long walks and had deep conversations. He felt recognized by his uncle who treated him as an equal. However, when he showed his "masterpiece" to the school authorities, he was roundly criticized for its over-the-top quality. Once again, his expectations of extraordinary recognition and greatness met with humiliation. The plot of this masterpiece combined bloodshed and ghosts, yearnings for death and yearnings for love. In listening to his detractors, Wagner decided that his work could only be judged rightly if it were provided with music.

Throughout his creative life Wagner argued that the poetry, the libretti he wrote have to carry the plot was as important as his music. Perhaps he was still trying to undo the injury his writings as a child had brought him. I'll come back to this point later.

Wagner's biographer, Newman (1946) writes:

> From the age of 14 on, Wagner borrowed money as he needed it, from friends and acquaintances on the ground that he thought himself, with some justice, entitled to financial support, private or public, in order that he might have the leisure and comfort necessary for him to produce masterpieces for the world.
>
> (pp. 48–49)

By the age of 17 Wagner dropped out of school and turned toward music. He decided not to go to University but to Music School, but

66 Childhood trauma and creativity

what really seemed to have attracted him were the dueling challenges and the gambling of the students.

Directly and indirectly, I have proposed that violating expectations in a variety of guises was a central theme in Wagner's life. He practiced it in his music and relationships. He callously betrayed the trust of his friends, would borrow money from them and would "borrow" their wives and return neither.

Mayes and Cohen (1996) have summarized the literature on expectancies and disruptions in expectancies in social interaction in the background of children exposed to early traumatization or who were otherwise considered to be at risk. "Out of the daily routines of being cared for, infants develop expectations for their parents' behaviors— the familiar touch, sound of the voice." Against this background, what is unexpected gets attention. Familiar touch and sound were both problematic for Richard Wagner. His mother rarely "caressed" him and his skin condition may have made him, at times, averse to touch. I have already spoken of the loud sound level in the Wagner home.

"Children, growing up in chaotic, inconsistent homes ... may be indiscriminate and unpredictable in their social relatedness" (p. 136). These observations have led Mayes and Cohen to hypothesize that the violations of expectations in early life may curtail and interfere with these children's "ability to feel safe and secure with others or when alone, to enjoy reciprocity, or to be able to endure normal frustrations, in short, to anticipate familiar scenes and tolerate the unexpected" (p. 136). Mayes and Cohen's hypothesis is clearly born out in the life of Richard Wagner.

In an autobiographical essay quoted by Newman (1946), Wagner wrote,

> What particularly attracted me to the theatre by which I mean also the stage itself, the rooms behind the scenes, and the dressing rooms—was not so much the desire for entertainment and distraction, as it is with the theatrical public of the present day, but the provocative delight of being in an element that opposed to the impressions of everyday life an absolutely different world, one that was purely fantastic, and with a touch of horror in its spell. I felt that contact with [this world] must be a lever to lift me from the

Childhood trauma and creativity   67

commonplace reality of the routine of daily life to that enchanting demon-world. It would make my heart beat wildly and fearfully.

(pp. 39–40)

In his provocative delight in participating in a different, fantastic world, opposing the impressions of everyday life, being lifted above the commonplace, Wagner acknowledges directly and consciously his delight in violating everyday expectations.

By the time he was 20 years old, Wagner had written his first opera *Die Feen* (*The Fairies*), and by the age of 25 he had composed *Rienzi*. Although this opera is now rarely performed, its Overture is frequently heard at concerts. The opera is set in imperial Rome; its plot however reflects Wagner's quasi-revolutionary leftist political views.

YouTube Videos
Overture to Rienzi
Overture to The Flying Dutchman
Overture to Lohengrin

Tannhauser and *Lohengrin* followed. In *The Flying Dutchman*, as Grout (1947) spells out, the turbulent stormy sea music is not just descriptive

of the sea but ... filled with descriptive meaning for the human drama. In the story of the redemption of the Dutchman from the curse of immortality ... Wagner for the first time clearly worked out of salvation through love which becomes fundamental in his later operas.

(p. 378)

YouTube Video
Wagner Overture to The Flying Dutchman

During the preparation of the production of *Lohengrin* a political upheaval in Saxony forced Wagner to flee to Zurich. Due to his political stances, Wagner could not return to Germany for 11 years. It was during this time that he wrote his virulently anti-Semitic treatise, *Judentum in der Music, (Judaism in Music, 2012)*. In it he attacked

Jews in general and the composers Meyerbeer and Mendelsohn in particular. I will have more to say about this treatise in the final chapter, "Music and the Jews."

While Wagner lived in Paris, Meyerbeer provided him with money and work. Wagner may have seen this as his due and felt little gratitude. In fact, Wagner could not tolerate Meyerbeer's success with the production of his opera, *Le Prophete*. That Meyerbeer was a successful composer, wealthy banker, and a Jew was difficult for Wagner to tolerate. Furthermore, Wagner also considered the death of Felix Mendelsohn in 1847 of benefit to him. He considered Mendelsohn style to be too conservative and thereby cramping the development of German music. In his treatise he proposed that Jews should annihilate themselves (or convert) because in their Jewishness they undermine the German language.

Alex Ross (2020) points out that a recurrent theme in Wagner's opera *The Flying Dutchman* as well as in the Ring cycle is trading women for gold. Ross attributes this to Wagner trying to lay bare corruption. Sure, but the gold is also linked to money and, as became clear in his antipathy toward Meyerbeer, to the Jews.

Operatic plots invariably challenge the credulity of the audience. Usually this occurs in the heat of passion, either fate dooms lovers, or chance, and "bad luck." Wagner, however, goes a step further. He relies on myths and miracles to violate expectations. The "miracle" in *Tannhauser* entails an inert walking stick that sprouts leaves. In the opera, Tannhauser has fallen under the sway of the sexual Venus and has abandoned the virtuous Elizabeth. Tannhauser confesses his sins to the Pope, Elizabeth dies and as Tannhauser kneels besides her, a band of pilgrims appear. They carry that walking stick that has sprouted leaves, a sign from the Pope that he has pardoned Tannhauser's carnal desires, and he has been redeemed.

YouTube Video
Wagner—Karajan—Tannhauser

Wagner, however, was even more gifted in his ability to violate the musical expectations of his listeners. The *Prelude* to *Tristan and Isolde*, which I will now discuss again, serves as an example. We are teased

Childhood trauma and creativity 69

with a never-resolving chord progression at the beginning of the prelude and onward. The chords do not get to their final resolution, the consummation of the love-death between Tristan and Isolde, until the closing bars of the opera.

Tristan has been sent by his friend, King Mark, to bring Isolde from her home to be his bride. She is despondent about entering a loveless marriage and because she loves Tristan, she wants to drink a poison potion with him so they can die together. Her maid substitutes a love-potion instead and that leads to all kinds of trouble. The tale of Tristan and Isolde has been told in various forms since medieval times with the motivations and the responsibility of the lovers presented in varying ways. For Wagner, Tristan and Isolde loved each other even before they drink the love-potion which does not so much cause them to love but rather causes disregard of societal mores and restraints. The libretto of *Tristan and Isolde* thus echoes a prominent theme in Wagner's life. He elevates betrayal of trust and friendship to heroic proportions and excuses the betrayal as a consequence of uncontrollable passions. And redemption comes after death. Let's listen to the love-death from *Tristan and Isolde* again, but now sung.

YouTube Video
Tristan und Isolde—End of Act 3—Liebestod

The works of Wagner that would be considered monumental and that clearly best illustrate the creative transformation of the character traits derived from his childhood experiences are the just-discussed *Tristan and Isolde*, the four operas comprising *The Ring of the Niebelungen* and *Die Meistersinger*.

In a moment, the story of Meistersinger, but first a digression about Wagner's relationship with Hanslick as relevant to Wagner's anti-Semitism. Hanslick was a powerful and feared music critic in Vienna. However, Hanslick had praised Tannhauser and called Wagner "the greatest living dramatic talent" (Newman, 1946, p. 30). Wagner thanked Hanslick in a long thoughtful letter and all was well until 1850 when Wagner published a virulent attack "Jews in Music." Offended and betrayed, Hanslick, also Jewish, then turned against Wagner. We are now at the time when Wagner was writing *Die Meistersinger*.

Before falling out with Hanslick, Wagner had already conceived of one of the opera's main characters, Beckmesser, as the pedantic, unimaginative judge of the song-contest held by the Meistersingers. Wagner then changed the name of that character to "Hanslich" and read the libretto to a group that included Hanslick. Hanslick stormed out in a rage. Wagner later renamed the character Beckmesser again. Once Hanslick became his enemy, Wagner went to great lengths to humiliate him in the opera. Beckmesser was initially costumed as a Hassidic Jew, a custom that was altered only in the last decades in productions of the opera.

In *Die Meistersinger*, on a grand scale, Wagner avenges himself against Hanslick and all his critics. In addition, in response to the criticisms of his music, Wagner constructed the opera along the academically prescribed model of the structure of a "master" song, as had been the musical traditions that the Meistersingers upheld. This was a tour de force in its own right.

Wagner depicts Beckmesser as the villain in the opera. He is depicted as a narrow-minded pedantic Jew, and a sneak and thief. At the conclusion of the opera, he is resoundingly humiliated. Wagner thus gives vent to both his rage at his detractors and his virulent anti-Semitism in one fell swoop.

There are two heroes in *Die Meistersinger*, the young Walther von Stolzing, and the mature Hans Sachs. Walther is brash, impetuous, creative, and a bit undisciplined. He defies conventions. He claims that he has had some musical training from the German minnesinger, Walther von der Vogelweide, but considers himself to be a "natural" musician and is quite self-satisfied with his musical accomplishments. Hans Sachs, a cobbler, and one of the Meistersingers, is wise, kind, and cautious, an ideal self-sacrificing mentor and "father figure." He is an upholder of conventions and traditions but also open minded. After hearing Walther sing, Sachs asks himself how Walther could have such extraordinary musicianship. He answers his own question: Like a bird's, the talent is natural. Both characters depict Wagner: Walther as Wagner saw himself and Hans Sachs, as he wanted to be seen by others. In these two personifications Wagner is also being both the father he wished he had had and the son who benefits from having had

Childhood trauma and creativity 71

such a wise, guiding, protective, and encouraging father. There was an actual Hans Sachs, an author, cobbler, and Meistersinger who lived in Nuremberg from 1494 to 1576. So, Wagner is also laying claim to a prestigious musical lineage for himself in the course of the libretto.

Die Meistersinger contains two pivotal scenes centering on violations of expectations, one toward the beginning of the opera and one at the end. The opera opens with Walther chancing to see Eva in church. The very first scene sets the stage for the violations of expectations that follow. In the church, as the congregation devoutly sings a hymn, Walther sees, flirts with, and falls in love with Eva. Wagner inserts their flirtatious sensual longings between the lines of the hymn.

YouTube Video
Wagner Die Meistersinger An Introduction
Wagner—Die Meistersinger von Nürnberg, Act 1

Walther learns that Eva is the daughter of a Meistersinger and that her father will give her hand in marriage to the winner of the song-contest that the Meistersingers will hold. Since only a Meistersinger may enter the contest, and since, so far, the only other applicant, is Beckmesser, Walther decides to audition to become a Meistersinger. To do so, he must improvise a song according to strict rules of musical structure, rhyme, meter, and rhythm, in accordance with the Meistersinger tradition. These were the "rules" that Wagner adhered to in composing the entire opera.

Walther will be judged as to his compliance with these rules. And here comes another violation of expectations. It is expected that the applicant will choose a text from the Bible as the subject of the improvised song. Walther thinks of Eva, and to the dismay of all, sings of love. Beckmesser, his rival for Eva's hand, turns out to be the judge who has to grade the singer according to his adherence to the rules. And he applies the rules assiduously. Walther sings creatively but not according to the rules. As he sings, Beckmesser tabulates Walther's "errors" by noisily running a piece of chalk across a blackboard. Walther accumulates more than the seven permissible errors and flunks the audition.

Wagner *Die Meistersinger*
Walther's audition

Based on his training and arrogance (his name, "Stolzing," contains the word "stolz" which means "pride"), he did not expect to fail. Here is the violation of expectations that provides the motivation for much of the opera. It is inflicted on the hero in a state of "archaic grandiosity" by an "academic conventionality" that does not recognize a "creative genius." A narcissistic blow! Walther wants to run off with Eva but Hans Sachs wisely dissuades him. In fact, Hans Sachs counsels Walther wisely throughout the opera.

In the course of the opera Walther has a dream about Eva, which he recounts to Hans Sachs who writes it down. The scene is like a psychotherapy supervisory session with Walther reporting his dream and Sachs writing it out with comments and criticisms as to how to make it acceptable to the establishment, to The Meistersingers. Sachs helps Walther fashion his dream into a song that he can sing at the contest.

The vindictive, sneaky, cheating Beckmesser, however, finds the paper on which Sachs had written Walther's song and accuses Sachs of planning to enter the contest himself. Sachs denies this and gives Beckmesser the paper with the words to Walther's song. Beckmesser leaves gloating. He is now set up for his ultimate humiliation.

In the final act, at the song-contest, Beckmesser, not having learned the song sufficiently, sings a ludicrous version of it and makes a fool out of himself.

YouTube Video
Meistersinger Act 3
Beckmesser's Humiliation

Sachs now leads Walther to the podium to sing his song. This time the Meistersingers and the people of Nuremberg are stunned. Having undergone a transformation throughout the opera, Walther now shapes his creativity in a more disciplined way.

YouTube Video
Walther's Vindication,
Prize Song

Childhood trauma and creativity   73

Walther wins the contest and therefore the hand of Eva, The Meistersingers now want to award him membership in the Meistersinger guild. Having won the hand of Eva, which was all he really wanted, Walther von Stolzing responds by telling them he can be happy without becoming a Meistersinger. Hans Sachs again counsels him not to disparage the Meistersingers, the upholders of German art and culture Walther accepts membership in the guild and Eva's hand. Here was another violations of expectations: Walther rejects the Meistersingers, and perhaps following Freud's dictum, Walther adjusts, but under protest.

To be a violator of expectations defined Wagner both in his art and his life. His early near-death experience that shocked his family through his survival, and the surprising emergence of his musical talent contributed to his expectation that he be treated as "special." He considered himself "entitled" to be given whatever (or whomever) he wanted and to be exempt from the rules that govern social behavior. Like his hero, Walther von Stolzing, Wagner liked to consider his talent to be "natural" and that the conventions of society were as ludicrous as were the rules established by the Meistersingers for their improvised songs. Like Walther von Stolzing, who guided by Hans Sachs, followed the rules to win Eva, Wagner had no Hans Sachs-conscience. He ran off with and impregnated Cosima, the wife of his friend, the conductor Hans von Buelow. That was the perverse side of Richard Wagner. But in his composition, the dialectic between tradition and innovation defined his creativity.

I have proposed two kinds of trauma in Wagner's childhood: His mother's report that he had been so ill that she almost wished he were dead would constitute a "shock" trauma, and the nagging question of his paternity might constitute a "strain" trauma. The early "near death" experience embellished and perpetuated by family lore became an organizing theme in his life: the expectation that he was above the laws of ordinary mortals. I propose that, like other creative artists who had "near death" experiences, having cheated death once, having violated the expectation that he would not survive, he elevated flaunting standards, betraying trusts and confidences, and expecting to be celebrated by one and all, into a way of life. His creative output in general and Meistersinger in particular illustrates this shock-trauma derived theme. The ongoing background doubt about his paternity, or rather the shame he associated with having been born to a potentially Jewish father, the strain-trauma of his youth required another solution. In Meistersinger he finds it by humiliating the Jewish father and critic in the person of Beckmesser and inventing for himself a pure German lineage dating back to the natural talent of the minnesingers, the German troubadours, and the kind solid, wise Hans Sachs. What could be better?

Chapter 5

Richard Strauss

Creativity in crisis and crises in creativity

On April 30, 1945, the day on which Adolph Hitler committed suicide, the 103 Infantry and Armored Division of the U.S. Army took possession of the German Alpine resort of Garmisch-Partenkirchen. Two hundred allied bombers were readied to attack this town and its environs. The town was host to a German army battalion but until then, the war had hardly touched it. In the nick of time, the German commander of the town surrendered, and the coordinated attack was called off.

Later that morning an American army security detachment was dispatched to requisition a house in Garmisch-Partenkirchen that would be used as headquarters for the American command. The American officer assigned to this task found a Garmisch villa that looked like it could well serve as a command post. The officer went inside and was greeted by an elderly gentleman, who with a smile, said to the American officer, "I am Richard Strauss, composer of *Der Rosenkavalier*." The American officer smiled back and said, "I am Milton Weiss pianist at the Jewish summer resorts in the Catskill mountains." Weiss posted an "Off Limits" sign in front of Strauss's villa and chose another house for the command post. Crisis averted (Ross, 2007).

Strauss, 85 years old by then, told Weiss about his troubles during the war years, about his Jewish relatives, his Jewish daughter-in-law, her parents, and her children, Richard Strauss's grandchildren.

Strauss would live for 3 more years in Garmisch. Between the year of his birth in 1864 in Munich and his death in Garmisch in 1948, he also spent some time in Vienna. That time and his writing *Der Rosenkavalier* make him, in my mind, an honorary *Wiener*. During

DOI: 10.4324/9781003220954-6

his lifetime he wrote glorious music and also encountered numerous crises, many of his own making.

Creativity can be born in crises, but crises do not necessarily foster creativity as Philip Roth, the American author has asserted. Pierpont (2013) tells that Roth spent considerable time with Czech writers after the communist regime had taken over and he argued that the repressive system that had characterized Czechoslovakia did not produce masterpieces. Rather it created coronaries, ulcers, alcoholism, depression, bitterness, and insanity. However, I believe that an artist who was able to create masterpieces in times of crisis had been prepared to do so by life experiences, prior to the crisis. And I believe that this was true of Richard Strauss.

During his formative years, Strauss developed an ability to balance compliance and defiance toward harsh authorities beginning with his father. Franz Strauss was a bitter, irascible, and abusive man and his mother, Josephine, was meek and nervous. She eventually went insane and had to be institutionalized, so wrote the musicologist, Alex Ross (2007). To this family description, Ross added that their son, Richard, was like many survivors of troubled families, determined to maintain a cool, composed façade behind which weird fires burned. Just how weird we will soon see and hear.

From this account I infer that Richard was raised by a very present father and an emotionally absent, but probably benign, mother. Franz Strauss was a horn player in the Munich court orchestra and he gave 6-year-old Richard his first lessons in composing music and playing the piano. Music may thus have become a special bond between father and son. It was destined to play a major role for Richard Strauss as an emotional resource and connection to the more available parent.

When Richard was 8, his father's cousin, Bruno Walter, later the conductor of the New York Philharmonic, gave Richard violin lessons. By age of 12, Richard had written his first composition. It was played by a symphony orchestra at that time. So far only compliance, no evidence of defiance yet.

Two experiences are critical in understanding Strauss's early creativity. At the age of 14, Richard went on a hiking vacation in the Alps. When he returned, he played recollections of his hikes on the piano. His talent for painting musical pictures resurfaced in many of his later

Creativity in crisis, crises in creativity 77

compositions. It enabled him to retain contact with the beauty of a bygone age. Already at age 14, Richard anticipated his mature style of combining lyrical romanticism and harsh realism, glorious-lush melodies that harkened to a beautiful past with dissonances that provide clues as to his then current life. And was he depicting the relationship between his stern father and his soft mother?

Many years later, in 1915, at the age of 51, Strauss drew on his youthful hiking experience and wrote his *Alpine Symphony*. In his music he captures the sparkling waterfalls and the rustling trees.

YouTube Video
Alpine Symphony

Strauss was, however, able to turn crisis into creativity when, at age 26, he came down with pleurisy. He was sent to Greece to recover and upon his return, he composed the tone poem *Death and Transfiguration*. Sixty-two years later, lying on his death-bed, Strauss said "dying is exactly the way I wrote about it in *Death and Transfiguration.*"

YouTube Video
Richard Strauss—*Tod und Verklärung*

To back up a bit, when Strauss was 44 years old, he composed a work that signaled his talent to the world and made him a celebrity. It was the tone poem *Don Juan* and it revealed much about him. It opens with a horn fanfare, perhaps a tribute to his father.

Strauss's *Don Juan* is the same Don Giovanni who goes to hell in the Mozart opera. Strauss however depicts his outlaw spirit in bounding rhythms and abrupt transitions. Simple melodies soar over sharp dissonances.

YouTube Video
Don Juan

Strauss's heroic *Don Juan* fares better than Mozart's scoundrel and signals an ongoing theme in Strauss's work and life: implicit and at times explicit admiration for an exploitative, autocratic authority.

Generally, Strauss could keep his feelings to himself and then let them escape, quite successfully, in his music. On the surface *Don Juan* and the later *Horn Concerti* were a musical tribute to his father but the music tended toward dissonance, exactly the music to which his father objected. Already then, this style came to characterize his music. His musical creativity resided in his extraordinary emotional expressivity, expressed through a juxtaposition of bold dissonances and gorgeous melodies.

Mozart had already experimented with dissonance, but Strauss, like his contemporary Gustav Mahler, made them an integral part of his music. Mahler juxtaposed his dissonances with contrasting trite-sounding simple melodies and Strauss played them off against gorgeous melodies and waltzes. Both composers captured the ominous underpinnings of their cheerful-appearing sociopolitical times.

In his relationships with authorities throughout his life, from his father to Hitler, compliance and defiance vied for expression. Strauss's complicated relationship to authorities characterized his life from childhood onward.

Initially, Strauss's defiance was well contained in his music. After 1933, when Strauss was 64 years old, came the rise of Hitler and the Nazis. The delicate balance between defiance and compliance that Strauss had been able to nurture and sustain became very shaky. In turn, that teetering balance created the crises that were at times in the foreground of his life and the background to his music. At times these themes were embedded in the libretti for his operas.

Generally, however, as Alex Ross (2007) described him, Strauss was a withdrawn man who kept his feelings to himself but they dominated his tone poems and made themselves heard in his 1904 *Symphonia Domestics* in which we hear sound coming from every room in the house, including the bedroom.

YouTube Video
Symphonia Domestica

Richard Strauss's early affinity for the music of Richard Wagner was a way of defying his father. Recall that Franz Strauss played in the orchestra of the court. That was the court of King Ludwig II, who was Wagner's main patron and who built the Festspielhaus in Bayreuth solely for the performances of Wagner's operas. However, Franz Strauss was a fierce musical conservative and had little use for Wagner's music. The then adolescent Richard complied with his father's prejudice and reassured his father that in 10 years no one would know of Richard Wagner.

As we shall see, Richard Strauss started to make ill-advised pronouncements very early in his life. Many years later the renowned conductor, Hans von Bulow, referred to Richard Strauss as Richard III because of the extent to which Strauss's orchestrations were inspired by Richard Wagner, Richard II.

In spite of Richard Strauss's initial mild defiance of his father's musical conservatism, a defiance that later became fortissimo, he wrote with affection about his father in his notebooks. Furthermore, with his father in mind, he wrote two horn concerti. And in Strauss's extensive use of the French horn in his orchestrations, we can hear his affectionate bond with father. From Strauss's history I infer that his father, probably the typically stern German father in that culture, was Richard's main functioning parent given the mother's depression and later hospitalization. Perhaps this chronic family crisis prompted the subtle defiance Richard expressed in his music and libretti, given his father's conservativism. Perhaps here was the source of Strauss's creativity. Through music he was able to connect with his father, defy his father through dissonance, and carve a path for self-expression. Ironically, we will see that for Cole Porter, composing music served similar functions—compliance and defiance of authorities and self-expression.

The early 1900s were highly productive years for Richard Strauss. He composed several of his greatest operas and tone poems during this time.

Tone poems are exactly what the term connotes. They are short, concise, well-structured compositions like poems. Rather than words they use melodies. We have already sampled two of these tone poems, *Don Juan* and *Death and Transfiguration*. We can now hear another one, *Til Eulenspiegel's Merry Pranks*. Remember the opening horns in *Don Juan*, well *Til Eulenspiegel* has them too. And the themes are in some ways quite similar. Till Eulenspiegel, a character from German folklore, and Don Juan, both defy conventionality. Till Eulenspiegel is beheaded for his pranks at the end of the tone poem and Strauss in his music, graphically depicts his head rolling away in the music. Let's hear the opening of *Till Eulenspiegel* and then the bouncing head at its finale.

YouTube Video
Strauss Till Eulenspiegels lustige Streiche

During these years Strauss's operatic output also flourished his first opera, *Guntram*, premiered in 1894, followed in 1901 by the premier of *Feuersnot*. Strauss wrote the libretti for both but neither was a success. However, the third one, *Salome* was a triumph.

In the first two operas Strauss experimented with Wagnerian territory. Guntram, a troubadour, rebels against the despotic Lord Robert, falls in love with Lord Roberts's wife and kills Lord Roberts in self-defense. Actually, Lord Roberts's wife reciprocates Guntram's love but he turns her down because he feels guilty and still has aspirations to become a saint. Strauss tried out a variety of endings for this opera, but they didn't seem to help much.

Max Graf (1946), a musicologist, a member of Freud's circle, and the father of Freud's poster-boy for the Oedipus Complex, Little Hans, wrote about *Guntram*. He ascribed to Freud's opinion that this libretto is a repression complex turned into an opera. Somehow Strauss must have gotten wind of Graf's interpretation because in his next opera, *Feuersnot*, Strauss satirizes Wagner's oft-used theme, "redemption through love." In Wagner's operas it is always women who, through their love, sacrifice their life, so that a man may rest or die, in peace, Strauss's version is "redemption through sex" and no one dies.

In *Feuersnot*, Kunrad, a sorcerer arrives in town at the time of the traditional eve of St. John bonfires. He is attracted to a young girl, Diemut, and kisses her in public. She offers to bring him up to her room in a basket. However, she just pulls him halfway up and leaves him hanging. In retaliation, Kunrad extinguishes all the bonfires in town. The only way to restore the fires is for him to have a virgin in heat. Diemut is persuaded to yield to Kunrad. She has her first sexual experience (which the orchestra depicts) and the fires are restored. Kunrad and Diemut emerge singing a love song.

Creativity in crisis, crises in creativity 81

These libretti illustrate that opera plots can be pretty outrageous. But two themes do emerge that will reappear in numerous future Strauss operas: autocratic authorities don't fare too badly and sexuality does very well. And this brings us to the third opera in this early group, *Salome*.

In these developing years, not only was Strauss's musical life characterized by his audacious, joyful exuberance, but there was also a touch of weirdness in his choice of setting Oscar Wilde's play, *Salome* to music. It illustrates Alex Ross's comment about Strauss's weird private side.

The plot of *Salome:* King Herod, the husband of Salome's mother, wants Salome to dance for him. He promises to give her anything she wants. Salome does her famous "Dance of the Seven Veils" and then, for payment, Salome demands the head of Jokanaan, the saintly Christian disciple whom Herod had locked up in his dungeon. Jokanaan had infuriated Salome's mother by calling her an adulteress and also had rejected Salome's seductive attempts. The head is bought to Salome on a silver platter and she makes quite a show of kissing the severed head. That's more than what Herod bargained for, and he orders his soldiers to kill Salome.

YouTube Video
Salome Dance of the Seven Veils
Final Scene

At the premier of *Salome* in 1906, among those in the audience was none other than Adolph Hitler. Later Hitler told Strauss's son that he had to borrow money to come to Graz in Austria to attend the premier of *Salome*. But after Hitler came to power, performances of *Salome* were banned.

Salome was followed in 1909 by the equally bloody *Elektra* in which there is already one corpse before the curtain even goes up. Before it comes down there are at least three more.

To maintain a connection with her murdered father, Elektra is intent on preserving his memory. She is ecstatic when her murdering mother is killed. Elektra then begins to dance and at the climax of her dance she falls dead.

There is a theme implicit in these operas that Strauss elaborates in his future work and life: a begrudging acceptance of despotic, exploitative,

82 Creativity in crisis, crises in creativity

and autocratic authorities. Lord Roberts is betrayed by his wife and, rightfully, attacks the betrayer. Kunrad succeeds in bedding a virgin, Herod is a bit lustful, kissing is ok, but kissing a dead head is weird, Elektra tries to keep Agamemnon honored memory alive after he is murdered by her mother for sacrificing Elektra's sister just so he could succeed in war. And there will be more.

We have already become familiar with the leading role played by the horn in many of Richard Strauss's compositions, his tone poems, and his concerti. It again plays a leading role in his great opera *Der Rosenkavalier* that we will hear shortly.

Growing up, Richard may have preferred to hear his father play the horn than to be exposed to other sides of him. With respect to his seriously depressed mother he may have wished to hear her voice more often and tried to preserve memories of times when she sounded less depressed. Dan Stern (1985) writing about the children of depressed mothers noted that some turn toward self-regulation in the absence of an interactive regulating mother. I think music provided a connection with his father, his affinity for the soprano voice may have provided a connection with a wished-for mother as well as a self-regulatory attempt to fill in for his emotionally absent mother.

Young Richard may even have heard his mother's voice on some occasions and tried to preserve the experience or wished he had heard it more often. He made writing for the female voice, for sopranos, a specialty and wrote breathtaking music for it.

Richard Strauss married a soprano, perhaps to preserve the best sounds from his home and to embellish and perpetuate them. Perhaps he is like those children who come from troubled homes who try to hang on to remnants and reminders of the best of their parents while they simultaneously try to dissociate the problematic aspects of them. This may add to the place of music in Strauss's life: to redo what was, to perpetuate the best, and to substitute his vision of what could or should have been for what was never there. Composing music served as a way of mastering both what felt enjoyable and what felt threatening. Music served as a way of negotiating some troubling times in Strauss's life. That would be one way of looking at his actions from 1933 onward. But I don't want to get ahead of myself.

Der Rosenkavalier had its premier in 1911 and is perhaps Strauss's signature work. Recall, that was how he identified himself to Milton

Weiss when the officer entered his home. It is, in my mind, not only a masterpiece but also a creative illustration of Heinz Kohut's paper on forms and transformations of narcissism. The opera illustrates Kohut's (1966) five transformation of archaic narcissism into its higher forms.

The libretto depicts an affair between an older woman, The Marschallin, and a young man, Octavian. She is called The Marschallin because she is the wife of the Field Marschall, who, for the entire opera, is away on maneuvers. If he had hung around, there would be no plot.

The Marschallin's boorish country cousin, Baron Ochs, enters and announces that he plans to marry a young girl, Sophie, and wants The Marschallin to arrange to have a nobleman, a cavalier, deliver the silver rose to the young bride-to-be. The custom of sending a silver rose to announce one's intention to marry is pure fiction, invented by Strauss's librettist, Hugo von Hofmannsthal. The Marschallin sends her young lover, Octavian, to deliver the rose and he and Sophie fall in love at first sight. The rest of the opera deals with untangling Sophie from Baron Ochs and untangling Octavian from The Marschallin.

Here is how Heinz Kohut's (1966) five transformations of archaic narcissism enter the operas. He posited that archaic narcissism, by which he means a kind of childlike self-centeredness is transformed in the course of favorable life circumstances or psychoanalytic treatment. It can be transformed into empathy by which Kohut meant an ability to understand another person by feeling oneself into their experience, creativity, wisdom, a sense of transience, and a sense of humor.

The central character, The Marschallin, has a sharp sense of humor, on the ironic side. Her humor becomes apparent already at the rise of curtain. The Marchallin and her young lover Octavian awake in bed. The Overture that has just preceded, depicts their lovemaking quite graphically, orgasms and all. When the curtain rises, Octavian says to The Marschallin who is lying next to him in bed, "the way you were, the way you are, nobody knows, nobody can even surmise it." to which The Marschallin responds, "Do you want everyone: to know?"

YouTube Videos
Strauss Der Rosenkavalier—Overture and the opening scene
Nein Neun (No I don't drink wine)
Leopold wir gingen Och's exit (Leopold we're going)
The Trio of Three Sopranos

84   Creativity in crisis, crises in creativity

Clearly, The Marschallin has (1) a sense of humor, (2) has wisdom because she knows about life, love, and the ways of men and women. She also has (3) a sense of transience and as older woman, gracefully relinquishes her lover Octavian to young Sophie in the finale, though, as the librettist puts it, she has a smile with one eye and a tear in the other. She also has (4) empathy. She senses what has transpired between Octavian and Sophie. For the finale of the opera, The Marschallin, Octavian, and Sophie, all three sopranos in different registers, join for one of the most glorious trios in all opera to which I referred earlier but we will soon hear it again.

But, before we hear it, a bit more plot. Octavian, the male hero is sung by a mezzo soprano. Strauss used the character of Cherobino from Mozart's *Marriage of Figaro* as a model for what is referred to in opera as a "pants role," a female singer playing the part of a young man.

When Baron Ochs arrives unexpectedly and Octavian should not be found in The Marschallin's bedroom, to protect The Marschallin's reputation, Octavian disguises himself as The Marschallin's maid, Mariandl. Now the mezzo-soprano has to sing as though she is a man disguised as a young woman. Baron Ochs, although planning to marry Sophie, now becomes infatuated with Mariandl and tries to seduce her. In the last act he takes her to an Inn and tries to get her drunk with wine. She fends him off by singing "No, no I don't want any wine."

YouTube Video
Nein nein

Try to keep that little tune in mind as you hear the closing trio because Strauss uses the same melody but has transformed it brilliantly.

At the finale, the three sopranos The Marschallin, Octavian, and Sophie sing a trio in which each expresses love, regret, longing various forms of loyalty, and renunciation. Sophie's father, a widower, appears and The Marschallin leaves with him. The implication is that most likely he will be her next lover. Octavian and Sophie can now express their love for each other without interference or encumbrances.

So, the character of The Marschallin is the embodiment of empathy, humor, an acceptance of transience, and wisdom. And the fifth transformation, creativity? That is the whole opera itself.

Creativity in crisis, crises in creativity   85

But there is more, the libretto depicts the plight of women when faced with the boorishness of some men. Unlike the tragic operas of Strauss where the women generally end up dead, *Rosenkavalier* is the quintessential depiction of an older generation of women protecting and paving the way for the next generation so they will not have to go through the humiliating and tragic experiences with men to which the prior generation was subjected.

Here, again is the theme of an older boorish man attempting to impose himself on a young girl, on both Sophie and Mariandl. But this time it's the women who triumph. But even though Ochs is humiliated at the end, Strauss's music does not send the scoundrel off in disgrace. He makes his exit in quasi triumph, in glorious waltz time.

YouTube Videos
Och's Exit
The Three Sopranos

What would have attracted Strauss to this theme of almost celebrating men who exploit vulnerable young woman? Did he retain some sympathy or compassion for them? For his father? Don Juan? Kunrad? Agamemnon, Herod? Ochs?

The years between 1933 and 1945 were filled with crises for Strauss. His son, Franz, had married a Jewish girl, Alice, and they had two sons who were of school-going age during the war. Alice's parents were sent to Auschwitz where, in spite of Strauss pulling all kinds of connections to try to save them, including driving there by himself, they eventually perished. Alice was arrested by the Gestapo several times and his grandchildren were bullied in school and were forced to spit on a group of Jews who had been gathered by Nazis. Then those Nazis spit on the two Strauss children.

These years clearly were difficult ones for Richard Strauss. And these crises provided an ever-present, well-documented background for Strauss's creative work from 1933 on.

Strauss and Hitler had a complicated compliance–defiance relationship. When Hitler came to power in 1933 Strauss proclaimed, "Finally a German Chancellor who likes art." When Hitler formed a government-controlled division of culture, Strauss became the head of its music division. Its mission was to rid German music of

86   Creativity in crisis, crises in creativity

Jewish composers and conductors. Until then, Strauss had admired Mendelssohn's music in particular, and could not understand why his music was to be banned.

In 1933 Strauss wrote in his private notebook "I consider the Streicher-Goebels Jew baiting a disgrace to German honor—the basest weapon of untalented, lazy, mediocrity against a higher intelligence and greater talent."

At the same time Goebels wrote in his diary "Unfortunately we still need Strauss, but one day we shall have our own music and then we shall have no further need of this decadent neurotic."

Strauss attempted to navigate a torturous path between staying in the good graces of the Nazis, allegedly in order to protect his family and protect his music, and his diffident attitude toward the Nazi regime. Other musicians left Germany, such as, Kurt Well, Erich Korngold, and Arnold Schoenberg. They found a welcome reception for their music on Broadway and in Hollywood, but Strauss stayed. He could not bear to leave his home in Garmisch. During World War II, when the German army requisitioned his home to use for war-injured soldiers, he objected. He stated that these soldiers did not get their injuries for him, and he had nothing to do with the war. To no avail, he was eventually forced to open his home to some injured soldiers.

During these war years, the Festival of Richard Wagner operas continued in Bayreuth. German officials swarmed there, and it was beloved by Hitler who was a regular attendee. Arturo Toscanini had been invited to conduct but he refused. He was staunchly anti-fascist. Strauss, however, volunteered to take his place. And when Bruno Walter was banned from conducting at the festival for being a Jew, Strauss took his place as well. Later a story surfaced that Toscanini had actually asked Strauss to pinch-conduct for him, for the sake of the music. Well, maybe? But this is hard to believe since Toscanini is quoted as having said, "To Strauss the composer I take off my hat. To Strauss the man, I put it back on again."

However, during these war years Pauline Strauss, even more than Richard, made their anti-Nazi views known. Nevertheless, stories of Strauss as "Nazi-sympathizer" followed him even though, in 1945, the American Denazificatiom Board cleared him. Yet, the reputation as having a questionable moral character clung to him. Strauss's argument that he was cozying up to the Nazis to protect his daughter-in-law and grandsons never seemed to diminish the label of collaborator that stuck to him. Strauss strove to remain apolitical but that is a tough stance to maintain when politics affect every aspect of daily life.

I believe that Strauss's apparent political stance grew out of his initial compliance–defiance relationship with his father. It worked well there, and Strauss argued that he survived under two previous regimes, he will survive again now. The only thing Strauss had going for him with the Nazis was that they needed to show him off as evidence of high German culture.

Strauss was not a loyal party member. He never joined the party and refused to give the Hitler salute. Yet after the war, he was criticized by the remaining world for having been a Nazi-sympathizer and collaborator. During the years, after the Nazis assumed power, Strauss tried to avoid politics and devote his time to writing glorious music. In fact, his devotion to his art was his *raison d'être* all along, for being a "bystander" as he was depicted by the Nazis.

Strauss's opera, *Dte Schweigsame Frau, The Silent Woman*, premiered in 1935 and was written in collaboration with the Stefan Zweig. Zweig was a Jew, hence his name was to be omitted from the advertising billboards for the opera. Strauss insisted that Zweig's name appear, and it did. Goebels complained that there were four Jews associated with the opera. Among the Jews, he included Ben Johnson from whom the original idea for the libretto was taken. Hitler and Goebels refused to attend the premier and the opera was banned after its first performances.

The Silent Woman a comic opera about a rich, rigid, intolerant man who is encouraged to marry a young, silent woman to take care of him in his old age. A mock marriage is arranged with actors employed to deceive the rigid, intolerant man. Another instance in which an authority figure is deceived and defied.

At the time he was composing *Die Schweigsame Frau*, Strauss wrote a letter to his librettist, Stefan Zweig. He wrote that in his composing he was not guided by any thought that he is German. Do you think, he asked, that when Mozart wrote he thought I am an Aryan? The letter was intercepted by the Gestapo and sent to Hitler. Strauss was dismissed from his post as president of the ReichsmusicKammer, the government music division he had headed.

And yet in 1936 Strauss composed the Olympic Hymn for the famous Berlin Olympics, the ones in which Jesse Owens upended the myth of Aryan superiority.

When it came to writing music, no matter for what occasion or who asked him, Strauss could not say "no."

YouTube Video
Olympic Hymn

To bring the creativity of Strauss to a close, I will return to *Der Rosenkavalier*. Among its highlights are its waltzes. The opera takes place in 18th-century Vienna when the waltz was just beginning to gain popularity but not among the aristocracy. The word waltz comes from the description by the nobility of how the peasants' dances appeared to them. To the staid nobles the peasants looked like wallowing pigs; the German word for "wallow" is "waeltzen." The nobles would not waltz but rather dance stately courtly dances. In the opera The Marschallin, Sophie, and Octavian do not have waltz music associated with them, but we do hear waltz music at the inn to which Ochs has lured Mariandl to have his way with her. And remember that Octavian had disguised himself as Mariandl. As Mariandl he or she could be connected to waltz music.

Max Graf (1946), recalled having taken a walk with Strauss. They passed a tavern from which waltz music emanated. Graf was surprised that Strauss stopped to listen. The music was badly played, and Strauss commented to him how the base line was way off. Graf then reports that Strauss used that very same base line in the waltz music he composed for the musicians who played at the inn to which Baron Ochs had taken Mariandl in *Der Rosenkavalier*.

To end this survey of Richard Strauss's creativity what better way than watch him conduct his glorious waltzes from *Der Rosenkavalier*.

I suggest whether you are reading this sitting down or lying down, whether you are alone or with company, you join Richard Strauss as he conducts the waltzes from *Rosenkavalier*, and dance. It is how this music is meant to be enjoyed, with one's whole body.

YouTube Video
Waltzes from *Der Rosenkavalier*
Conducted by Strauss

Chapter 6

Cole Porter

Trauma and self-restoration

At the age of 45, just after returning from a walking tour in Europe with two friends, Cole Porter stopped in Paris to see his wife, before she returned to their house in the states. Cole and Linda had an argument. She was still angry with him for not better concealing his homosexuality. After an attempt at a reconciliation, Cole returned to New York where the score of *You Never Know* awaited his final touches.

Soon after arriving, Porter accepted an invitation from his old friend Tookie, better known as the Countess di Zoppola, to spend the weekend at her country house in Great Neck, New York. There he did what he most enjoyed, arrange for a party to go horseback riding. He saw a horse that appealed to him and although warned by a stable hand that this horse was particularly skittish, he nevertheless insisted on riding it. Galloping through the woods, something spooked the horse. The horse fell and rolled over Cole Porter's legs. Both of his legs were crushed and soon an infection of the bone marrow set in. Wracked in pain, Porter lay, pinned down by the horse, awaiting someone to rescue him.

From early childhood on, Cole Porter had been raised not to depress his friends by revealing his pain or discomfort to them. His mother raised him with the admonition that a gentleman does not depress his friends.

While waiting to be rescued, as he lay beneath the horse in excruciating pain with crushed legs, Porter told his friends that he took out his notebook and worked on a song he had been composing that still needed a verse. The song was "At Long Last Love."

DOI: 10.4324/9781003220954-7

YouTube Video
Lena Horne Sings At Long Last Love
https://youtu.be/4KZbP8QhTl8

When I told this story to various friends, including some psychoanalysts, I was invariably asked, if I believed the story. That's not the point. Whether Cole Porter literally took out his notebook, thought about taking it out, or made up the whole story afterwards, is not the point. What Porter "claimed" speaks to how he tried to restore himself after his painful fall and as he lay helpless in a debilitated state. In the story he reminded himself of who he was, who he had been, and who he wanted to continue to be, in spite of the pain and suffering he was now undergoing. No matter how hopeless and helpless he felt, he was still Cole Porter, composer and lyricist.

The story, whether or not it actually occurred, describes Porter's attempt at self-restoration. In working on his song he reminded himself that he was still Cole Porter. No doubt, Cole Porter's story was also influenced by his mother's admonition not to depress his friends.

To me, the more interesting question would be, what function would that story have served for Cole Porter? And here is where my title, "The Self-Restorative Power of Music" applies. This story also reminded me of the self-restorative power music provided for my family and by extension for me, when we fled from Germany.

Two themes that organized Cole Porter's life are already evident here. He kept his depressed, painful feelings to himself. Well, as we shall see, more or less. And he was able to exercise a powerful sense of determination. The importance to Porter of music in defining and reinforcing his sense of self will become evident as we look at his life and upbringing.

Cole Porter's strong will was shaped in the cauldron of his domineering grandfather and his pressuring family. He was the only surviving grandchild in a very, very wealthy family. This made him the target of diverse, contradictory expectation from his mother and his grandparents.

His great-grandfather, A. A. Cole, had moved from Connecticut to Peru, Indiana, in 1834, where his son, James Omar (J. O.) Cole, grew

92 Trauma and self-restoration

up. During the gold rush of 1849, J. O. moved west to make his fortune in California. It turned out that indeed he did make a fortune. But it was not in gold, it was in the dry goods business. He then invested this money in farmland in Indiana and in timber, coal, and oil in West Virginia. The timber land he had bought turned out to be rich in coal and oil. At that time J. O.'s wealth was estimated to be $17 million.

J. O. Cole was the father of Katie Cole who married Samuel Porter, a druggist who also played the piano and sang. The Cole side of the family was financially driven, amassed lots of money, but showed no musical talent. The Porter side, at least this was true of Samuel, was quite laid back. Some might even have called Samuel "passive" as we shall see, with respect to his involvement with his son. But Samuel was likeable and charming.

The dynamics of Cole Porter's family: consisted of an intrusive over-protective mother and a passive father. This family constellation would have been utilized in the psychoanalytic literature of the 1950s and 60s (for example, Socarides, 1977) to account for Cole's homosexuality, I raise that issue in order to set it aside as simplistic (Lachmann, 1975). Porter's sexual orientation was a multifaceted issue in his life, I do not intent to account for it on the basis of his having been raised by his particular parents. I take his sexuality as a "given" as was his musical ability and the cleverness and creativity that infused his lyrics.

The enormous family wealth was partially responsible for setting Cole apart from other children as he grew up. But Cole would later say that the money did not spoil his life, but rather made it very comfortable. In the family conflicts about how Cole was to be raised, Katie, Cole's mother, weighed in by approving of Cole riding horses. However, she specifically forbade him to play football or other such sports. She considered them ungentlemanly. She directly approved of Cole learning to dance, and he was also tutored in French. And, most important, she directly encouraged his musical interests.

Cole did make friends with boys and girls in his school, friendships that were formed around a mutual fascination with the circus which came to town periodically.

The adults in Cole's life, his mother, and his grandparents had strong, very firm opinions as to how Cole should be raised and specifically how he should be educated. His grandfather wanted Cole to become

Trauma and self-restoration **93**

a lawyer. Indeed, when the time came, Cole applied to, and entered, Harvard Law School, at least briefly. Everyone was opposed to Cole studying music although he was given piano and violin lessons from about age 5 onwards. His mother did eventually support his study of music. When Cole was 10 years old, he and his mother wrote a musical together. His father stayed out of the entire decision-making process.

The disputes between Katie and her father with respect to how Cole should be raised continued throughout Cole's life. Cole's grandfather insisted that he remain at their home in Indiana and attend schools there. But Katie, who succeeded in getting away from home to attend schools in Connecticut and New York, supported her son and she prevailed. However, in defying his grandfather Cole risked jeopardizing what would be his enormous inheritance.

From Cole's perspective the risk may not have seemed so great. It certainly did not influence his musical interests. It appears that from an early age onward, music infiltrated Cole's identity. It certainly cemented his relationship with his mother.

The family quarrel lasted for several years during which Katie and her father did not speak to each other. Cole went off to boarding school in Connecticut and rarely came home to visit his family nor did they visit him. For Cole, this family quarrel served to sharpen his determination to face and attempt to overcome obstacles placed in his path.

When he was 13 years old, Cole was enrolled at Worcester Academy in Connecticut. He arrived there lugging his piano, among other possessions. We don't know what else Cole brought but to bring an upright piano to his school indicated how crucial music had become for him. It connected him with his mother and simultaneously defied his grandfather's autocratic control over him and the family.

By then, Cole had been studying piano for 7 years and had become very proficient. He quickly became known, accepted, and even sought after, as a pianist at the academy. He also tried out to be pitcher for the baseball team. No success. But as a member of the glee club he was a star.

Dean Abercrombie, dean of students at the Academy, had a lasting, and for Cole, a memorable influence on him. As an adult Cole credited Dean Abercrombie for helping him to realize that he was able to match

94 Trauma and self-restoration

the rhythm of his words to the beat of his music (McBrien, 1948). From Worcester Academy he went to Yale.

As an undergraduate at Yale, Cole joined several student singing, performance, and dramatic groups. He both performed in and wrote music and lyrics for their shows. The witty writing style that made him famous can already be seen to emerge. He wrote clever and "naughty" songs and gathered much adulation. Typical were the lyrics and music he wrote for a show by one of the Yale musical societies, Dramat' Smokers. For their show *Kaleidoscope* he composed a song and lyrics in which he rhymed *"sword of Damocles" with "Box of Rameses."*

In his late 20s Cole Porter was hospitalized for a urinary tract infection and tested positive for syphilis. Treatment, before the discovery of penicillin, was arduous. We know about this hospitalization since Porter wrote about it to Boris Kochno with whom he was in love. In one of his numerous letters to Kochno, who was just leaving for Naples, Cole wrote,

> as for your departure, I am trying to console myself by thinking of your return, but it's quite difficult. And the only thing I really want to do, is to climb on top of the bell tower and announce to the piazza that I am desperately in love (literally in the original French, I am in love to the point of dying) with someone who has taken this evening's train to Naples and that I am going to follow him … Oh there's nothing to say Boris, I love you so much that I think only of you—I see only you and I dream only of the moment when we'll be reunited. Goodnight darling. C
>
> (McBrien, 1948, p. 93)

From his urinary tract infection and syphilis we can assume that Porter had not been living a celibate life, although the identity of the men he loved becomes better known after Kochno. Earlier in his life, Cole Porter and his life-long friend Monty Wooley, frequented a house of male prostitution in Harlem. As was the case for many of the love songs that Porter wrote to express his love for a man but written as though intended for a woman, he wrote a song about how he yearns for his "Harlem Wench."

During the years when Cole was in love with Boris Kochno, he was married to Linda, who, not so incidentally, brought her own fortune with her. She had been recently divorced from a man who treated her quite brutally. However, she left the marriage with a million dollars. Biographers of Cole and Linda debate whether Linda was aware of Cole's homosexuality when she married him and that she married him on condition that he keep it concealed. After her abusive marriage, Linda may well have been repelled by sex, as some commentators speculated. Others referred to her as a very nice woman but very naïve. Still others described Cole and Linda's relationship as mother and son. After all, she was 8 years older than Cole. And some authors speculated that Linda tolerated Cole's homosexual affairs as he did Linda's lesbian encounters.

At about this time he wrote a song that made a direct overt reference to homosexuality, which was very unusual for him. The song is about a woman who goes to the movies with a man and says to him that she likes the actor John Gilbert and then asks him whether he likes him too. She then realized that he felt very similarly about John Gilbert.

In his early 1930s Cole Porter took a cruise down the Danube with Eddy Tauch, who, a friend of Porter claimed, "was the great love of his life" (McBrien, 1948, p. 154). Then in his mid-30s, Porter composed the music and lyrics for *Anything Goes*. His song "You're the Top" ends with "But if, baby, I'm the bottom You're the top." Numerous commentators have described this ending as Porter inserting his sexual preference into the song. However, many composers of the day wrote parodies of that song. That last couplet may well have been written by Porter's friend, Irving Berlin. Nevertheless, *Anything Goes* was a rousing success. It was top form Porter and his reputation already stellar by then, was reinforced manyfold.

YouTube Video
You're the Top from Anything Goes
Ethel Merman and Frank Sinatra
https://youtu.be/Vc7152gQK-U

In 1935, the Porters moved to Hollywood for part of the year. But Linda Porter liked Hollywood far less than Cole. Apparently, Cole concealed his homosexuality even less there than in New York. That offended Linda.

96 Trauma and self-restoration

Among the advantages of living in California was that Cole could go horseback riding there as often as he liked. Porter even told his friends that "he would rather compose on a horse than on a piano" (McBrien, 1948, p. 193).

The next show on which Porter worked was *Jubilee* that featured a song, "Down in the depths on the nineteenth floor." It contained a couplet that even the janitor's wife has a good love life. That line was felt to be in bad taste and so Porter changed it to "even the analyst's wife has a perfectly good love life." That change already reflected Porter's attitude toward mental illness and its treatment, as will become evident later when he became clinically depressed.

By 1937 Cole and Linda's marriage had become strained. Cole liked living in Hollywood where he became more part of a homosexual community. Linda felt the loss of Cole's companionship and left for Paris. That was when Cole went on a walking tour with two friends, Eddy Tauch, "the love of Cole's life," was one of them.

Upon his return, Cole went to Paris and found Linda still angry and returned to the states without her. Soon after he arrived, he found the invitation from Tookie to weekend at her country house. Cole mounted that skittish horse for a ride that changed his life forever.

Cole enjoyed horseback riding and, recall, it had been one of the activities that was sanctioned by his mother.

Porter's biographers (McBrien, 1948) attribute his story about taking out his notebook as he lay crushed beneath the horse to his need to avoid being the object of pity and not depress his friends as his mother had raised him. George Eells (1967) ascribes the story to Porter needing to remain the invincible youth who moved from one triumph to another. This accident would put an end to Porter being able to cling to that identity.

Focusing on his music, enabled Porter to persevere and preserve himself. As though he felt, I cannot allow my precious self to be crushed. So he restored himself by reminding himself that, no matter what, he is still Cole Porter.

Cole Porter's story reminded me of the mother who, when my friends and I were attacked by the Nazi youths in the park, suggested that we all pee in the street. The act had no connection or relationship to what had just occurred to us, but it was symbolic. It reminded us that we were still intact. Similarly, Porter claiming that he took out his notebook had no direct connection to his fall and being crushed by the horse. It symbolically reinforced his sense of who he was before the fall. Both acts were restorative, designed to calm and convey a sense of intactness and going-on-being.

There is yet another aspect to his holding on to his identity as a composer. The lyrics of many of Porter's songs, although love songs that a woman can sing to a man, or vice versa, were composed by him as love songs to a man in whom he was interested. His music provided him with a surreptitious expression of his sexual longings and love. In the lyrics contained in his music, Porter could express and conceal his sexuality at the same time. The music and the lyrics that they contained were essential to his expressing and simultaneously concealing his love life.

While still in Paris, Linda began to make plans to divorce Cole. However, when she heard of his accident she immediately returned to be at his side.

Following the accident, Cole Porter was in continuous pain. Some doctors advised amputating his legs, but Cole was opposed to that. Sometime later, one leg was amputated leaving him with continuing phantom limb pain. His pain required continuous medications. Each day he took 14 different narcotics, sedatives, and hypnotics. During these years he would be seen lying in his hospital bed with his eyes rolled back and beads of perspiration rolling off him. When he was able to return to his Waldorf Astoria suite where he and Linda lived, a big and elegant party was arranged. Unfortunately, Porter was still too drugged to appreciate it. Yet, a few months later, he began work on a new show. He had his piano raised so that he could play while sitting in his wheelchair.

As he was recovering in the hospital, Cole Porter was visited by his many friends, among them, Elsa Maxwell. In his drugged state he told her, "It just goes to show fifty million Frenchmen can't be wrong. They eat horses rather than ride on them" (McBrien, 1948, p. 212).

Cole told Linda that his work saved his life and makes him forget his pain. The music he wrote immediately after his accident was not considered to be top drawer but one show, *You Never Know* did contain "At Long Last Love." The song, Porter said, he was working on while trapped underneath the horse.

98 Trauma and self-restoration

As Cole was recovering, about a year after his accident, he tripped on a stair and broke his left leg. This put an end to his already limited mobility. He was then often carried by two men.

During the summer in 1938 Cole and Linda rented a house at a New Jersey beach. Linda was rarely there, and Cole used the house for his "trysts." As his relationship with Linda became more strained, Cole participated in what his neighbors described as noisy orgies involving many soldiers from a nearby army base.

The next show on which Cole worked, *Leave It To Me* was a hit. It starred two newcomers to the Broadway stage, Gene Kelly and Mary Martin who sang "My Heart Belongs to Daddy" which became her signature song.

To back up a bit, Richard Rogers (in McBrien, 1948, p. 141) tells of a meeting with Cole Porter. Porter told him that in order to write hit songs, he found out, he has to write Jewish tunes. And so he did. Prominent among these Jewish songs is, "My Heart Belongs to Daddy" with its "... dadadada daddy."

YouTube Video
Mary Martin Sings My Heart Belongs To Daddy
https://youtu.be/r404pTC_qGI

For the Broadway season from 1939 to 1940, the World War II years, Porter wrote five very successful shows, *DuBarry Was a Lady, Panama Hattie, Let's Face it, Something for the Boys*, and *Mexican Hayride*.

During these years Porter was writing and composing at a rapid clip. He was also increasingly feeling his loneliness and isolation. He had numerous friends who were not lovers and he had numerous lovers who never became the kinds of friends in whom Porter could confide.

In working on the score for *Something for the Boys*, Porter met and fell in love with the dancer and choreographer Nelson Barclift. Soon, Porter was sending love telegrams to him. "Thinking of you constantly, All Love, Cole" (McBrien, 1948, p. 249).

During these years Linda and Cole continued to live at the Waldorf Astoria in separate apartments. Cole continued to work and live, more or less, after his accident as he did before. He hobbled around on crutches and with braces on his legs. At times he would have to be carried, but essentially he continued to compose and write as he had before. Of course, composing and writing lyrics gave him a feeling of continuity as nothing else could have. It genuinely sustained him. And his sexual life seemed to continue as it had prior to the accident was probably similarly sustaining. The strength and fortitude that had been qualities of his grandfather, his critical and dictatorial grandfather, and the determination of his mother to fight for her son's independence, all joined forces in letting Cole address and surmount the challenges he now faced.

Cole Porter loved to travel, and his incapacity was not going to deter him from pursuing this passion. In early 1939, leafing through a *National Geographic* magazine he came upon an article on Machu Picchu. He was determined to see it and he spent the next few weeks learning Spanish, With Ray Kelly and Paul Sylvian to help carry him and assist in his personal needs, and his friend, Howard Sturges, Porter left for Peru.

Porter's mobility was severely impaired. He could move himself along by using two canes. He wore braces on both legs that went up to his hips. The climb up the mountain was arduous. Porter used crutches and a wheelchair. But Kelly and Sylvan had to lift him over rough terrain. Part of the trip had to be on horseback, which Porter was able to do. The assessment of Porter by his "handlers" was that he was "a person of great physical courage, sometimes verging on foolhardiness" (McBrien, 1948, p. 212).

There is no question that Cole Porter enjoyed taking on challenges. Having found a way of dealing with his physical restrictions, another challenge he had dealt with for many years, became more prominent. He now took on the censors who had "blue penciled" some of his lyrics. There was a bit more leeway for naughty lyrics on the Broadway stage than there was on the radio. Porter's next successful musical, *DuBarry Was A Lady* contained lyrics that did challenge the censors. And recall that Katie was also his mother's name.

YouTube Video
Katie Went to Haiti
https://youtu.be/pt8iPMwUqhs

During the World War II years Cole Porter carried on his own war with the puritanical movie and radio censors. Not even the word, "jerk" was allowed.

During these war years Porter continued to write and enjoy his circle of "celebrity" friends. Besides his lover, Nelson Barclift, there was Norma Shearer, Fanny Brice, Greta Garbo, and Ernst Lubitsch. But this circle of friends still left Porter without the companionship and romantic love that he sought. He suffered for much of his life lacking an intimate relationship. His friends were all, in some way, unusual people.

Porter's friend, Sam Stark, was married to the daughter of a Mafia boss in Kansas City. Once a month Stark would go to Kansas City and return with a suitcase filled with hundred-dollar bills. How much Porter knew of this is unclear, but Stark was a great traveling companion for Porter. At the parties Porter enjoyed attending at Lew Kessler's house, the host invited male guests to rummage through trunks filled with women's clothes and then appear in drag.

During these years, the Porter's marriage became increasingly strained. As they grew older, both had health issues (Linda had chronic lung disease) and their patience with each other diminished. In particular, Cole became less guarded about his sexual proclivities and that offended Linda.

In the years 1943 and 1944 Cole's tendency toward depression became more apparent. His crippling accident and the many medications he took were a contributing factor. But, in addition, a number of projects fell through, and he was not as busy as he had been during previous years. In 1935 Porter wrote a song for movie that was never made. The song was "Don't fence me in." In 1944 the song was revived by Porter and used in another movie, *Hollywood Canteen.*

YouTube Video
Roy Rogers Sings Don't Fence Me In
https://youtu.be/kg_zurRBHlg

Warner brothers planned to produce a film about Cole Porter's life in 1944. The idea for the film was suggested by Irving Berlin who believed that Porter's struggle with the aftereffects of his accident would prove inspirational to injured service men coming back from the war. The script that was written caused "... a number of screenwriters' (to) ... lamented the lack in Porter's life of 'struggle'." Orson Wells asked, "What will they use for a climax? The only suspense is—will he or won't he accumulate ten million dollars?" (McBrien, 1948, p. 290).

That "lack of struggle" was, more or less, what I thought as I read Porter's biographies and in writing this chapter. What brilliant lyrics, what clever music, what a sophisticated wit and what a superficial approach to life. His mother's admonition, "Don't depress your friends" may have had the effect of prompting Cole Porter to keep his feeling within and not reveal them. He did reveal his sexual and love feelings in an unconflicted way.

I thought about the other composers that I have discussed. Wagner and Strauss were very engaged with the people in the wider world in which they lived. Strauss's ambivalent relationship with Hitler is a case in point. That was a world in which life and death issues played out in real time. Cole Porter kept his struggle with his leg injuries quite private and the world in which he spent his life was the world of the Broadway musical. It was a world in which, almost no matter what, there would be applause before the final curtain.

While preparations for the production of the film based on his life were in progress, Cole spent considerable time undergoing more operations on his legs. And even more operations were expected in the future.

Alexis Smith was cast as Linda and Cary Grant was cast as Cole Porter—in spite of the enormous difference in appearance of the two men, but problems developed early on. First the writers did not know how to end the picture. Then Cary Grant complained, apparently with some validity, that the dialogue was poor and there was little characterization. And then there was the Hays Office, the movie censors, who required that such words as "gigolos," "hell," and "cocaine" not to be mentioned. And Porter's sexual proclivities were only hinted at, but in tune with the "morality" of the time, Porter was depicted as having the riding accident, not as it occurred, but on his way to meeting a lover, implicitly punishing him for his homosexuality.

Porter's next project was a production of *Around the World in 80 Days* with Orsen Wells. It was a flop, but it was followed in early in 1948 by what many believed was his best work, *Kiss Me Kate.*

Almost all the songs for that show were written by Porter in a state of excruciating pain. He was suffering from an ulcer, abscesses, and

102 Trauma and self-restoration

due to a bump, a part of his shinbone was exposed. The drugs he was taking did not reduce his enormous pain. Yet, while enduring all this pain, Porter wrote such songs as "We open in Venice," "Why Can't You Behave?" and "Brush up your Shakespeare"

YouTube Videos
Kiss Me Kate Medley
We Open in Venice
https://youtu.be/oGLlxuAPcjU
Why Can't You Behave
Always True to You in My Fashion
https://youtu.be/W3WGkx1MYDQ?t=106
Brush Up Your Shakespeare
https://youtu.be/bPduoU826ew

Linda's health had been deteriorating and she had great trouble breathing. Yet, she and Cole continued to smoke. Cole had to leave Linda in the hospital when he went to California to begin work on a new musical, *Out of This World*. One of the songs, "Nobody is Chasing Me" again brought Porter into conflict with the censors:

YouTube Video
Nobody's Chasing Me
https://youtu.be/ilzmpBJlnG0

It's not difficult to figure out which line the censor insisted should be deleted. Although on the heels of *Kiss Me Kate* the producers had no trouble raising money for this show, Porter felt little enthusiasm for the show. Perhaps, he sensed that it would not be a success. Perhaps, his physical condition was increasingly wearing away his determination to contain his despair within himself. His friends noticed Cole's black moods, fits of temper, and lack of appetite. He would have one string bean for supper.

For his 60th birthday, celebrations were scheduled at major venues throughout the country. Thousands were present at Yale Bowl for Cole Porter night, but he did not feel well enough to attend. He also suffered from insomnia and a strange new symptom: anxiety about his finances.

Trauma and self-restoration 103

During the 1950s Porter's anxiety about not having enough money persisted. He called his financial state "precarious." No amount of reassurance from his lawyers and accountant could diminish his anxiety. Had Cole harbored a childhood memory of his grandfather pointing out the poorhouse to him on their walks together? The implication had been that his grandfather predicted he would end up there.

When Linda next saw Cole, she was shocked by his appearance. He had lost weight and appeared in a constant state of anxiety. But both Linda and Cole were scornful and dismissive of psychology and considered psychotherapy a vulgar form of exhibitionism (McBrien, 1948). Shortly thereafter Cole went to Paris with his valet, Paul Sylvian. They had planned to stay for six weeks but returned after one week with Cole suffering from a severe depression, delusions, and suicidal. Cole was admitted to Doctors Hospital in New York and given electroshock treatments for a period of time. His depression diminished but his delusions about his lack of finances remained untouched.

By a year or so later, Porter's spirits seemed to have been restored and he began to work on his next musical, *Can Can*. Writing the music for that show was a stroke of luck. It gave Porter a chance to shift his attention again to the censors as his enemy. Just as writing, or imagining he was writing the lyrics for "At Long Last Love," helped Porter to pull himself out of his painful helpless state after the horse fell on him, he needed another musical to provide him with a similar source of self-restoration.

YouTube Video
Can Can
https://youtu.be/lmJk0tMEagk

Another show *Silk Stockings* followed and then the movies *Adam's Rib*, *High Society*, and *Les Girls*. During these years both his mother and Linda died leaving Cole without the encouragement and support he received from these two women. What did live long after the death of his mother was the stoicism she had engendered in him. Cole Porter had a pillow in his apartment embroidered with the legend, "Don't Explain; Don't Complain."

104   Trauma and self-restoration

Porter's health seemed to continue to deteriorate. He ate little, lost weight, began to withdraw from the theater life of which he had been so much a part. By the beginning of 1957 Porter was in a hospital again for a gastrectomy. And as the years went on, Porter's health and musical output both declined. In 1958 he wrote the music for a TV production of *Aladdin* and was hospitalized for treatment of his osteomyelitis. The show was a flop and the medical treatments not much better. A few months later his right leg was amputated at mid-thigh level. He was subsequently fitted with a prosthesis. He exercised diligently but with a feeling of hopelessness. Increasingly he withdrew into a sullen depression. *Aladdin* was the last show for which he wrote music, and his last song was, "Wouldn't it be Fun."

YouTube Video
Wouldn't It Be Fun
www.youtube.com/watch?v=Wk5

Cole's depression deepened and his life became more ritualized. A masseur arrived each morning who provided Cole with more than a massage, as was inferred from the extra money and lavish gifts Cole bestowed upon him. The physical and psychological deterioration continued. Cole ate very little. He invited friends for dinner but did not speak and was plagued by general pain, phantom leg pain, and incontinence. It was a tragic end for a man who prized clever turns of phrase and elegance, even fastidiousness in dress and appearance.

According to their biographies, Richard Wagner died in 1883, Richard Strauss died in 1948. And Cole Porter died in 1964. Truth be told, none of them really died. Like Beethoven and Bernstein, like Schubert and Sibelius, and many other composers, they all just turned into music.

Chapter 7

Finale
Music and the Jews

A complicated relationship between the music and the Jews has wound its way through many of the foregoing chapters. Jews have had an affinity for and a love of music, not only because of its important place in religious services, but also because music has the advantage of not taking up any physical space yet still occupies a sizable position in the quality of one's life. That makes music ideally suited for people who, every once in a while, must flee from their homes when a subtle ever-present anti-Semitism escalates into a pogrom or even a holocaust. Unlike one's belongings, money, and property that an Elfriede or a government tax can usurp, a love of music can be kept safely within oneself. My family carried music as a treasure from Germany to the United States for the enrichment of all of us. For my parents and their generation, hearing music, no matter how or where, provided an emotional continuity with the best of themselves.

It was surprising to my family, how available and free of charge classical music was in New York. Music was there. All you had to do was look for it or find it by chance. To a large extent, refugees from Germany certainly looked for it. I remember the extent to which I heard German spoken by attendees milling about during intermissions in the lobby at free concerts of the A.B.C. Symphony Orchestra and at Carnegie Hall concerts of the New York Philharmonic. Its very popular conductor was Bruno Walter, a German Jew. He was a distant relative, as I have discussed, of Richard Strauss and one of his teachers.

That so many Jewish music lovers ended up at concerts in New York is a paradoxical consequence of the Nazis having driven them out of the concert halls of Germany and the other European countries the Nazis occupied. Furthermore, as the biographies of Richard Wagner

DOI: 10.4324/9781003220954-8

and Richard Strauss and even Cole Porter illustrate, composers are quite susceptible to being influenced to compose music that reflects their attitude toward the Jews.

I have described Wagner's anti-Semitism as embodied by his villains in his operas, in the Ring cycle and in *Die Meistersinger*. In his treatise *Judaism in Music* (Wagner, 2014), which has been variously translated as "Jews in Music," "Jewishness in Music," "Judom in Music," and "Judaism in Music," Wagner elaborated in venomous detail his antipathy toward Jews. He attacks and dismisses Felix Mendelsohn as sweet and tinkling but without depth. His attack on Meyerbeer is more complicated. Meyerbeer had actually helped Wagner financially and artistically. He arranged for Wagner's early opera *Rienzi* to be performed. But Meyerbeer had two irredeemable flaws in Wagner's eyes. First, Meyerbeer's opera *Le Prophete* had been a success in Paris. Even though Meyerbeer had helped Wagner get *Rienzi* to be staged, Wagner resented Meyerbeer's popularity and did not like his music. Second, Meyerbeer was not only a Jew but also a rich banker. That combination may have been too much for Wagner to swallow.

In his treatise, Wagner also expressed his dislike for the sound and manner of the way in which Jews speak. The way in which the Jews "blabber" and "squeak" when they speak, he held, makes them incapable of expressing deep passion in song and music. To make matters worse, Wagner argued that the children of these Jews pretend to be able to speak European languages. However, since they cling to their father's language, their speech also emerges as "jumbled blabber."

This vicious side of Wagner's character stands in sharp contrast to operas in which he demonstrates a profound understanding of human nature, love, loyalty, and devotion. The contrast between these two, apparently irreconcilable sides of Wagner, fills much of the literature devoted to his life and work.

Wagner sets the "Jewish" blabber to music in *Die Meistersinger*. Beckmesser, costumed as a Jew, tries to sing his poorly learned version of the song that he had "stolen" from Hans Sachs and Walther von Stolzing. Wagner believed that the *Volk*, the people, are the arbiters of what constitutes genuine art. And hearing Beckmesser sing, they chant that he does not seem to be the right one. That is, the Jew is an imposter and cannot be a true representative of German art.

Finale: music and the Jews 107

All the while, the specter of probably being the son of a Jewish father hung over Richard Wagner. Prior to writing his treatise on Jews and music, Wagner came upon some letters written by his mother to him just before she died. In them she confirmed that he was Geyer's son. The connection between these letters and his writing the anti-Semitic treatise is pure conjecture.

In fact, Wagner had told Nietzsche earlier in his life that he believed that Geyer was his father. In that case he would not have needed his mother's letters to confirm it. His virulent anti-Semitism most likely dates back to a much earlier time. It was certainly rampant in the world in which he lived. In fact, it was the not-so-latent anti-Semitism that Hitler was able to stoke into a holocaust, a short time later.

In contrast, Richard Strauss did not disavow his Jewish family members. Having a Jewish daughter-in-law, and thus Jewish grandchildren, was handled quite deftly by him. The anti-Semitism of his day was also rampant and life-threatening as well. It clearly placed Strauss in numerous difficult circumstances. His world fame provided him with a certain degree of protection by making him a necessary and valuable presence for the Nazis. They needed him to be able to show him off. Yet, when his daughter-in-law's parents were sent to Auschwitz, Strauss drove there, on his own, to try to free them. He failed.

Although pressured to do so, Strauss never joined the Nazi party nor did he give the "Heil Hitler" salute. Yet, the label of "collaborator" clung to him after the war, I think, unfairly. Yes, he was guilty of accepting the title of head of the music chamber in Hitler's government. And yes, he accepted conducting assignments at the Festspielhaus in Bayruth when more outspoken anti-Nazis refused to conduct there. One of the conductors barred from conducting was Bruno Walter. And yes, Strauss wrote the hymn for Hitler's Olympic Games in 1935. It is more likely that Strauss would do almost anything to preserve and promote his music. And yes, he also collaborated with the Jewish author Stephan Zweig.

Going back to his relationship with his father, Strauss's early pattern of compliance and defiance was tested during the Nazi era. He complied, he argued, to insure his and his family's survival. However, his self-protective side and his impetuous qualities did not always cooperate with each other. Strauss's relationship with Stefan Zweig took courage as well as naiveté. Strauss did not seem to be aware that letters sent to Zweig would be opened by the Nazi censors. So, when he wrote to Zweig that he did not think of himself as a German composer, he was clearly courting a crisis. The libretto of the opera that he and Zweig composed entailed a defiance of an autocrat. Nevertheless, in spite of taking needless risks, he managed to survive the Hitler era and World War II and could greet Milton Weiss when the American officer chanced upon him to requisition his home.

By the time Cole Porter came on the scene, the Broadway musical world had changed. It seemed that the Jews whom the Nazis chased out of the opera and concert halls of Germany joined the Jews who had escaped from the pogroms in Eastern Europe not only to fill Carnegie Hall and the Metropolitan Opera, but also ended up as audiences for Broadway musicals. A number from *Spamelot* captured this well.

YouTube Video
David Hyde Pierce: If You Want to Have a Hit on Broadway
Spamelot

Cole Porter told Richard Rogers that until he started to write Jewish music his shows were flops (McBrien, 1948). By Jewish music Porter referred to Kletzmer style music and composing melodies in a minor key. Jewish music, generally being sad in tone and lyrics, as befits the Jewish experience, would generally be in a minor key.

George Gershwin has not yet been heard from. His inclusion of Jewish music is prominent in the Kletzmer clarinette solo that begins his Rhapsody in Blue and his use of a Hebrew prayer as the music for "It aint neceesarily so" in Porgy and Bess. Later composers, like Sheldon Harnick, continued that tradition in *Fiddler on the Roof.*

The effect of anti-Semitism has turned out to be paradoxical. It has forced Jews out of Eastern Europe and German-speaking countries and deposited them into the cultural life of the United States, just one of the countries to which they fled. Based on the experiences of my family and me, I have focused particularly on the presence, impact, and contribution of Jewish and gentile composers to music in America. Irving Berlin who wrote both *God Bless America* and may have written a couplet for Cole Porter's "You're the Top" led the list

Finale: music and the Jews 109

of the Jewish presence in music in the foregoing chapters. Leonard Bernstein as both composer and musicologist played a major role in these chapters, but George Gershwin has not yet been mentioned nor have a host of other Jewish composers. But I did not intend to write about Jewish composers, per se. Rather I want to explore the relationship between Jews as music consumers and the music they consumed. I wanted to write an alternative perspective to Wagner's anti-Semitic essay on Judaism Music.

Wagner wrote how Jews detract from music and I want to write first about how music enriches life and how Jews, by their very engagement with music, are keeping a love of music and musical traditions not only alive but thriving.

I would like music to have the last word in this book about music. If in the course of reading these chapters the reader will have listened to some great works perhaps only briefly, not in their entirety. How about listening to them now. And I suggest that you also listen to Leonard Bernstein conducting Beethoven's Ninth Symphony from beginning to end. Or, why not watch one of the operas I have written about. Only then will I be comfortable to say, "Curtain."

References

Beebe, B., & Lachmann, F. M. (2002). *Infant research and adult treatment: Co-constructing interactions*. Hillsdale, NJ: The Analytic Press.

Beebe, B., & Lachmann, F. M. (2015). *The origins of attachment*. New York: Routledge.

Bernstein, L. (1976). *The unanswered question*. Cambridge, MA: Harvard University Press.

Bernstein, L. (1982). *Findings*. New York: Simon & Schuster.

Bulluck, P. (2011). *To tug at the heart, music must first tickle the neurons* (pp. D1–D4). Science Times, New York Times, April 19.

Coriat, I. H. (1945). Some aspects of psychoanalytic interpretation of music. *Psychoanalytic Review*, 32, 408–418.

Crewe, O., Nagel, F., Kopiez, R., & Altenmueller, E. (2007). Listening to music as recreative process: Physiological, psychological, and psychoacoustical correlates of chills and strong emotions. *Music Perception,* 24, 297–314.

Crewe, O., Kopiez, R., & Altenmueller, E. (2009). The chill parameter: Goosebumps and shivers as promising measures in emotion research. *Music Perception,* 27, 61–74.

DeCasper, A., & Carstens, A. (1980). Contingencies of stimulation: Effects on learning and emotions in neonates. *Infant Behaviour & Development*, 9, 19–36.

Eells, G. (1967). *Cole Porter: The life that late he lived*. New York: Berkley Publishing Corp.

Graf, M. (1946). *Modern music*. New York: The Philosophical Library.

Grout, D. J. (1947). *A short history of opera*. New York: Columbia University Press.

Greenson, R. R. (1954). About the sound 'Mm …'. *Psychoanalytic Quarterly*, 23, 234–239.

Haas, K. (1984). *Inside music*. New York: Anchor Books, Doubleday.

Hadley, J. (1989). The neurobiology of motivational systems. In J. Lichtenberg (Ed.), *Psychoanalysis and motivation*. Hillsdale, NJ: The Analytic Press, pp. 227–372.

Haith, M., Hazan, C., & Goodman, C. (1988). Expectations and anticipations of dynamic visual events by 3.5 month old babies. *Child Development*, 59, 467–497.

Irvine, D. (1911). *Wagner's bad luck*. London: Watts & Co.

Jaffe, J., Beebe, B., Feldstein, S., Crown, C., & Jasnow, M. (2001). Rhythms of dialogue in infancy. *Monograph of the Society for Research in Child Development*, 66(2), pp. 1–141.

Klein, G. (1950). Freud's two theories of sexuality. In L. Breger (Ed.), *Clinical-cognitive psychology, models and integration*. Englewood Cliffs, NJ: Prentis Hall, pp. 136–151.

Kohut, H. (1957). Observations on the psychological functions of music. In P. Ornstein (Ed.), *The search for the self: Selected writings of Heinz Kohut: 1978–1981* (Vol. 1) Madison, CT: International Universities Press, pp. 233–254.

Kohut, H. (1966). Forms and transformations of narcissism. In P. Ornstein (Ed.), *The search for the self* (Vol. 1). Madison, CT. International Universities Press, pp. 427–460.

Kohut, H. (1968). The psychoanalytic treatment of narcissistic personality disorders – Outline of a systematic approach. In P. Ornstein (Ed.), *The search for the self* (Vol. 1). Madison, CT. International Universities Press, pp. 470–510.

Kohut, H. (1971). *The analysis of the self*. Madison, CT: International Universities Press.

Kohut, H. (1977). *The restoration of the self*. Madison, CT: International Universities Press.

Kohut, H. (1981). Introspection, empathy, and the semicircle of mental health. In P. Ornstein (Ed.), *The search for the self: Selected writings of Heinz Kohut: 1978–1981* (Vol. 4). Madison, CT: International Universities Press.

Kohut, H., & Levarie, S. (1950). On the enjoyment of listening to music. In P. Ornstein (Ed.), *The search for the self: Selected writings of Heinz Kohut: 1978–1981* (Vol. 1). Madison, CT: International Universities Press, pp. 135–158.

Lachmann, F. M. (1950). *The modern interpretation of Bach. Choir Guide*. November, pp. 50–52.

Lachmann, F. M. (1975). Homosexuality: Some diagnostic perspectives and dynamic considerations. *American Journal Psychotherapy*, 25, 254–260.

Lachmann, F. M. (2001). Words and music. In A. Goldberg (Ed.), *The narcissistic patient revisited: Progress in self psychology* (Vol. 17). Hillsdale NJ: The Analytic Press, pp. 167–178.

Lachmann, F. M. (2008). *Transforming narcissism: Reflections on empathy, creativity, and expectations*. New York: The Analytic Press.

Lachmann, F. M. (2010). Addendum: Afterthoughts on little Hans and the universality of the Oedipus complex. *Psychoanalytic Inquiry*, 30, 362–557.

References

Lachmann, F. M. (2014a). Mm, Mm, Good. *American Psychoanalyst*, 48(2), 18.

Lachmann, F. M. (2014b). Richard Wagner: Grandiosity, entitlement, and its metastases. *Psychoanalytic Inquiry*, 34, 498–511.

Lachmann, F. M. (2016). Credo. *Psychoanalytic Dialogues*, 26, 499–512.

Lachmann, F. M. (2019). Richard Strauss: Kreativitaet in Kriesenzeiten und Kreative Kriesen. In Goßmann, M. & Harms, A. (Eds.) *Kriese und Kreativitaet*. Frankfurt: Brandes & Apsel, pp. 285–296.

Langer, S. (1953). *Feeling and form*. New York: Charles Scribner's Sons.

Lichtenberg, J., Lachmann, F., & Fosshage, J. (2010). *Psychoanalysis and motivational systems: A new look*. New York: Routledge, Taylor and Francis Group.

Lichtenberg, J., Lachmann, F., & Fosshage, J. (2016). *Enlivening the self: The first year, clinical enrichment, and the wandering mind*. New York: Routledge.

Lyons-Ruth, K. (1999). The two-person unconscious: Intersubjective dialogue, enactive representation, and the emergence of new forms of relational organizations. *Psychoanalytic Dialogues*, 19, 576–617.

McBrien, W. (1948). *Cole Porter*. New York: Vintage Press.

Mayes, L. C. & Cohen, D. J. (1996). Playing and therapeutic action in child analysis. *International Journal of Psychoanalysis*, 75, 1235–1244.

McKee, R. (1997). *Story*. New York: Harper Collins.

Mithens, S. (2006). *The singing Neanderthals*. Cambridge, MA: Harvard University Press.

Newman, W. (1946). *The life of Richard Wagner*. New York: MacMillan.

Panksepp, J. (1995). The emotional sources of "chills" induced by Music. *Music Perception*, 13, 171–207.

Panksepp, J. (1998). *Affective neuroscience*. New York: Oxford University Press.

Panksepp, J. & Trevarthen, C. (2009). *The neuroscience of music*. New York: Oxford University Press, pp. 104–146.

Pierpont, C. R. (2013). *Roth unbound*. New York: Ferrar, Straus and Giroux.

Ross, A. (2007). *The rest is noise*. New York: Ferrar, Straus and Giroux.

Ross, A. (2020). Phantom vessel. *The New Yorker*, March 23, pp. 66–67.

Sachs, O. (2008). *Musicophelia*. New York: Vintage Books.

Siegmeister, E. (1945). *The music lovers handbook*. New York: William Morrow and Company.

Singer, J., & Fagen, J. (1992). Negative affect, emotional expression and forgetting in young infants. *Developmental Psychology*, 28, 48–57.

Socarides, C. (1977). *Homosexuality*. New York: Roman and Littlefield.

Stern, D. (1985). *The interpersonal world of the infant*. New York: Basic Books.

Stern, D. (1995). *The motherhood constellation*. New York: Basic Books.

Stolorow, R. D., & Lachmann, F. M. (1980). *Psychoanalysis of developmental arrests: Theory and treatment*. New York: International Universities Press.

Tronick, E. (2011). Infant's meaning making and the development of mental health problems. *American Psychologist*, 66(2), 107–119.

Wagner, R. (1983). *My life*, trans. A. Grey. Cambridge, UK: Cambridge University Press.

Wagner, R. (2014). *Judaism in music*. Menlo Park, CA: Aristeus Books.

Woodhead, J. (2010). Trauma in the crucible of the parent-infant relationship: The baby's experience. In T. Bardon (Ed.), *Relational trauma in infancy*. London: Routledge.

Index

Aaa sound 20, 25
Abravanel, M. 9
absolute music 43–44
Adam's Rib 103
Adorno, T. 25, 26
Aladdin 104
Alpine Symphony 77
Altenmueller, E. 33–34
American Broadcasting Company Symphony Orchestra 13, 105
anxiety-tension-reduction model of musical enjoyment 19
Anything Goes 95
aphasia 49–50, 54
archaic narcissism 83
Around the World in 80 days 101
"At Long Last Love" 90–91, 97, 103

Barclift, N. 98, 100
Beebe, B. 14
Beethoven, L. van 21–22, 24, 43, 44–49, 54, 55, 56, 104, 109
Berlin, I. 4, 95, 108
Bernstein, L. 16, 26–27, 104, 109; on Beethoven's *Ninth Symphony* 45–46; connections with individual students 9; on evolution of music 25, 30, 52; on mmm sound by babies 51; on music as pure emotion 11; on Stravinsky 25–26; study of music 19–22, 24; on tonality 25–26
Bizet, G. 13, 22, 30, 39, 54, 55
Blizstein, M. 10
Boston Symphony Orchestra 9
Brandenburg Concerto #3 47–48
Brecht, B. 6
Brice, F. 100
"Brush up your Shakespeare" 102

Can Can 103
Capriccio 42–43
Carstens, A. 23
Casablanca 44
Chabrier, E. 13
chill response 32–33, 37–38
Chomsky, N. 20, 52
co-construction model 21
Cohen, D. J. 66
Cole, A. A. 91
Cole, J. O. 91–92
Cole, K. 92
Crewe, O. 33–34

Das Rhinegold 42
Death and Transfiguration 77, 79
Debussy, C. 25
DeCasper, A. 23
Der Freischütz 60, 63
Der Rosenkavalier 8, 33–34, 75, 82–84, 88–89
Descartes, R. 10, 29
diatonism 25
Die Dreigroschenoper (The Threepenny Opera) 6, 10
Die Feen 67
Die Fledermaus 15
Die Meistersinger 8, 69–74, 106
Die Schweigsame Frau 87–88
Don Juan 77–78, 79
"Don't fence me in" 100
Doyle, A. C. 39
DuBarry Was a Lady 98, 99

Eells, G. 96
Eggert, M. 14
1812 Overture 43–44
8th Symphony (Schubert) 8

Elektra 81–82
emotional engagement: based on meeting, surpassing, or violating expectations 30, 35–37; chills and 32–33, 37; goose bumps 34–35; separation-distress-vocalization and 31–32; through music 29–30
Epstein, H. 10
España Rhapsody 13
"Every Time We Say Goodbye" 34

Fagen, J. 35
Feuersnot 80
Fiddler on the Roof 108
Fifth Symphony (Shostakovich) 35
Fifth Symphony (Tchaikovsky) 6
Firebird, The 26
Fleming, R. 43
Flying Dutchman, The 67–68
Fosshage, J. 20, 50–51
Foster, S. 9
Four Season, The 43
Fourth Movement 44
Franklin, B. 29
Freud, S. 15, 17, 18, 19

Garbo, G. 100
Germany: Jewish flight from 1–4, 105, 108–109; music in cultural life of 4–8; under the Nazis 1–5, 11–12, 75, 78, 85–87, 105–106, 107; under the Weimar Republic 5
Gershwin, G. 108, 109
Geyer, L. 58–61, 107
Gilbert, J. 95
Goberman, M. 13
God Bless America 4, 108
Goebels, H. 86
Goodman, C. 36
goose bumps 34–35, 55
Graf, M. 80
Grant, C. 101
Greenson, R. 19, 20, 24, 51–52
Guntram 80

Hadley, J. 22
Haith, M. 36
harmonic series 16–17
Harnick, S. 108
Hazan, C. 36
Herrmann, B. 36, 40
High Society 103

Hitchcock, A. 36, 40
Hitler, A. 1, 2, 4, 5, 75, 78, 81, 85–88, 101, 107
hmmmmmm sound 52, 55
Hollywood Canteen 100
Horne, L. 91
Horst Wessel Lied 3

"If You Want to Have a Hit on Broadway" 108
infant-adult conversation 23–24
infant research 20–21, 30; on mmmm sound by infants 51; on motherese 50–51, 53–54
Irvine 60
Ives, C. 19–20

jazz music 24
Jews: complicated relationship between music and 105–109; fleeing from Germany 1–4, 11–12, 108–109; life in Germany prior to the rise of Hitler 4–6
Jubilee 96

Kelly, G. 98
Kelly, R. 99
Kessler, L. 100
Kiepura, J. 14
Kiss Me Kate 101, 102
Klein, G. 17
Kochno, B. 94
Kohut, H. 26, 83; on centrality of sense of self 15; comparison of music to poetry 19; on listening to music as involving whole body 16; on music as play 19; on novel interfaces between music and psychology 18; on psychotherapeutic treatment as improvisational duet 18; on repetitions and rhythm in music 18–19
Kopiez, R. 33–34
Korngold, E. 86
Kubie, L. 16

Lachmann, F. M. 20, 50–51; on bonding with his father and enjoying music in New York 13–14; college music courses taken by 9; emigration of family of 1–3, 105; interest in psychoanalysis 10, 13–14; on music in Germany 4–8
La Marseillaise 44, 55, 56

116 Index

Lambeth Walk, The 3
Langer, S. 23
Leave It To Me 98
Lehar, F. 8, 14, 43
leitmotifs 42
Le Prophete 68, 106
Les Girls 103
Let's Face It 98
Levarie, S. 15
Lichtenberg, J. 20, 50–51
Lubitsch, E. 100

Ma, Y.-Y. 34–35
Mahler, G. 44–45, 78
Marriage of Figaro 84
Martin, M. 98
Ma sound 25
Maxwell, E. 97
Mayes, L. C. 66
meaning-making 40, 55
Mendelsohn, F. 68, 86, 106
Merry Widow, The 14–15, 22, 39, 43, 54, 56
Mexican Hayride 98
Miles, R. 25
Mithens, S. 30, 52–53
Mmm sound 19, 20, 24, 25, 51
motherese 50–51, 53–54
movie music 36–37, 40–41, 44
Mozart, W. A. 44, 77–78, 84
music: co-construction model of 21; complicated relationship between Jews and 105–109; cross-disciplinary study of 20; emotional engagement with (*see* emotional engagement); engaging the whole body 10–11, 16, 29–30; goose bumps and 34–35; improvisation in jazz 24; as language of emotions 30–31; meaning-making with 40, 55; memory and meanings attached to 14–15; movie 36–37, 40–41; as narrative (*see* narrative); oral gratification through 19, 20; origins of 53–57; poetry and 19, 22; psychology and 15–28; repetitions and rhythm in 18–19, 22–23; tonality in 17, 25–27; universals of 26–28
musicology 16–17
"My Heart Belongs to Daddy" 98

Nagel, F. 33–34
narrative 39–40; babies' mmm sound 51; Beethoven and 44–49; conversation,

dialogue, and the concerto in Beethoven's *Ninth Symphony* 47–49; motherese 50–51; movie music 36–37, 40–41, 44; music, affect, and 53–57; Oliver Sachs and 49–50; origins of music and 52–53; program music and absolute music 43–44; words and music in opera 41–43
Nazi Germany 1–5, 11–12, 75, 78, 85–87, 105–106, 107
Newman 65, 66–67
Nietzsche, F. 107
Ninth Symphony 44–47, 54, 55, 56, 109
Nutcracker Suite, The 6

Oedipus complex 14–15
Ol' Man River 49, 50
Olympic Games, 1936 88
"On the Meaning of the Sound Man" 19
opera, words and music in 41–43
oral gratification through music 19, 20
Out of This World 102
Owens, J. 88

Panama Hattie 98
Panksepp, J. 30–33, 51, 52, 54
Parkinsonism 50
Peer Gynt 8
"Philosophy of Modern Music, The" 25
Piano Concerto in G #4 24
Piano Trio in E Flat Major 35
Pierce, D. H. 108
Pierpont, C. R. 76
poetry 19, 22
Porter, C. 11, 34, 106, 108; anxiety and depression in 100, 102–103, 104; "At Long Last Love" 90–91, 97, 103; death of 104; family of 91–93; financial troubles of 102–103; health issues of 94, 104; homosexuality of 90, 92, 95, 96; life in California 95–96; loneliness and friendships of 98, 99, 100; marriage of 94–95, 96; musical training of 93–94; physical disability of 98–99, 101–102; private struggles of 101, 102–103; riding accident of 90, 97–98; self-preservation and restoration through music 96–97; travel despite being disabled 99
Porter, L. 90, 94–98, 100, 102–103
Porter, S. 92
Presall, D. 20

Index   117

procedural memory 24
program music 43–44
Psycho 36–37, 40–41
psychoanalysis 10, 13–14; listening to
   patients in 18; memory associations
   with music in 14–15

Queen Mary 1–3

repetition 18–19, 22–23
Rest Noise, The 35
"Rhapsody in Blue" 108
rhythm 18–19, 23; time and 25; vocal
   23–24
Rienzi 106
Rogers, R. 98, 108
Romeo and Juliet 22
Ross, A. 35, 68, 76, 78
Roth, P. 76

Sachs, O. 49–50, 54
Salome 80, 81–82
Schoenberg, A. 25–26, 86
Schubert, F. 8, 12, 35, 38, 104
sense of self 15
separation-distress-vocalization 31–32, 54
sexuality, Freud's theory of 17
Shakespeare, W. 22
Shearer, N. 100
Shostakovich, D. 35
Sibelius, J. 12, 34, 35, 37, 38, 104
Siegfried 60–61
Silk Stockings 103
Singer, J. 35
Sixth Symphony (Beethoven) 43, 44–45
Sixth Symphony (Tchaikovsky) 6
Smith, A. 101
Smith, Kate 4
Something for the Boys 98
Sonata opus 31, 21–22
Spamelot 108
Stark, S. 100
Stern, D. 23, 82
Storolow, B. 11
Strauss, F. 76, 78–79
Strauss, J. 8, 15
Strauss, P. 86–87
Strauss, R. 8, 11, 33–34, 42, 75–76, 105,
   106, 107–108; childhood of 76–77;
   death of 104; *Der Rosenkavalier* 8,
   33–34, 75, 82–84, 88–89; early
   creativity of 76–77; musical style of

78; *Olympic Hymn* 88; operas of
   80–82; relationship with Hitler and
   the Nazis 85–88, 101; Richard Wagner
   and 78–79; tone poems of 79–80
Stravinsky, I. 25–26
Sturges, H. 99
Sylvian, P. 99, 103
Symphonia Domestica 78–79
Symphony #2 34, 35, 55
Symphony in C 13, 22, 30, 39

Tannhauser 67–69
Tauch, E. 95, 96
Tchaikovsky, P. I. 6, 43–44
temporal continuity 11
Threepenny Opera, The 10
Til Eulenspiegel's Merry Pranks 79–80
time and rhythm 25
tonality 17, 25–27
tone poems 79–80
Toscanini, A. 86
Transfigured Night 26
Trevarthen, C. 30
Tristan and Isolde 17–18, 25, 68–69
Tronick, E. 39

Utah Symphony Orchestra 9

Vivaldi, A. 43
vocal rhythm 23–24
von Weber, C. M. 60

Wagner, C. F. 58–59
Wagner, J. 58–61
Wagner, R. 7–8, 11, 17–18, 25, 41–42,
   58, 101; anti-Semitism of 67–68, 105,
   106–107; autobiography of 59–60,
   64; chaotic home life of 60–61, 64,
   66–67; death of 104; *Die Meistersinger*
   8, 69–74; early brush with death 62;
   family of 58–59; musical training
   of 60, 62, 65–66; operas composed
   by 67–74; plays written by 63, 65;
   Richard Strauss and 78–79; unhappy
   childhood of 64–65
Walter, B. 76, 86, 105
Weill, K. 6, 9
Weimar Republic 5
Weiss, M. 75, 83, 108
Well, K. 86
Welles, O. 101
"We open in Venice" 102

118 Index

"Why Can't You Behave?" 102
Wooley, M. 94
"Wouldn't it be Fun" 104
WQXR radio 4, 9–10

You Never Know 90, 97

Zigeuner Baron 15
Zweig, S. 87, 107–108

Printed in the United States
by Baker & Taylor Publisher Services